Here's what some of skiing's top experts are saying about *WomenSki*

"This book is not just for women. It is for every man that skis with a woman, every ski instructor, and all ski shop employees. Claudia's easily understood perspectives are a valuable contribution to the sport of skiing."

—Warren Witherell and David Evrard
Authors of *The Athletic Skier*

"At long last, a book that will help women stand up on their skis and get involved with the sport. When I started skiing, it took a unique and feisty woman to be recognized as a knowledgeable skier. It still does. But, this book will help women claim their fair place on the slopes."

—Anna McIntyre, First woman officer of the
U.S. Ski Association and first woman Chief
of Alpine World Cup Races in the world

"*WomenSki* addresses the frustrations that prevent so many skiers from reaching their potential. Claudia empowers the reader by breaking down intimidating barriers, providing insightful tips and crusading for the athlete in all of us."

—Dee Byrne, PSIA Demo Team member
Instructor, Beaver Creek Ski School

"*WomenSki* has my full attention! Claudia covers crucial issues that are barriers to improvement that I had to overcome in my own skiing and that I see constantly as a ski instructor and coach. Coming from a true love of skiing, Claudia is telling women skiers NOT to settle for LESS and how to do so.

—Carol Levine, former PSIA Demo Team
member & Staff Trainer, Beaver Creek

"If you are female and you ski, this is essential reading. If you are male and want to understand women who ski, likewise."

—Diane Slezak Scholfield
Executive Editor, *Skiing America*

"Carbone makes the case that skiing is a sport, and perhaps a lifestyle, that clearly discriminates against her sex. But her responsive treatise is not a crusade, not a gripe session, not a litany of nonconstructive support-group sympathy for disgruntled female skiers. Carbone is a doer, not a whiner."

—Stu Campbell and Carol West-Campbell
Ski Magazine

Dedication

To John
who started it all by teaching me to ski

To Susan, David, Michael, Kathleen and Nick
for all the skiing memories

To Howie
for Aspen

and
To every woman who skis

by Claudia Carbone

World Leisure Corporation
Boston, MA & Hampstead, NH

Cover design by Tim Gilbert, Orange Slice Comm., Hampton, NH.

Illustrations by Laura Gharrity

Distributed to the trade in USA by
Login Publishers Consortium, 1436 West Randolph Street, Chicago, IL 60607; (312) 733-8228, (800) 626-4330.

Distributed to the trade in Canada by
General Publishing Co. Ltd., 30 Lesmill Road, Don Mills, Ontario M3B 2T6, Canada, tel. (416) 445-3333.

Distributed to the trade in Europe by Roger Lascelles,
47 York Road, Brentford, Middlesex TW8 0QP Tel. 081-847 0935.

Mail Order, Catalog and Special Sales by
World Leisure Corporation, 177 Paris Street, Boston, MA 02128. Tel. (617) 569-1966, fax (617) 561-7654

ISBN: 0-915009-32-3

Acknowledgments

To my brilliant publisher, Charlie Leocha, for "thinking like a woman" in order to appreciate the value of this book in the skiing world and bringing it to life.

To my gifted editor, Julie Hutchinson, for her experienced guidance, her encouragement, and her delightful enthusiasm. Thank you for making our sessions so pleasant and mutually enlightening!

To Warren Witherell, who kept my writing technically correct and provided me with a huge boost from the ski industry side.

To Dee Byrne and Carol Levine for the inspiration.

To Barb Sanders, Christie Smith, Alison Clayton, Jo Garuccio, Jamie Mackintosh, Brenda Buglione, Lisa Feinberg Densmore, Ashley Fischer, Nancy Luke, Patricia Simmons, Barbara Kester and Peggy Sax for their willingness to share their expertise as contributors to this book.

To Edna Dercum for being an amazing role model for women skiers.

To everyone who took time to talk with me about my favorite subject.

Especially, to all the women who eagerly shared their skiing experiences, good and bad.

Contents

Introduction

"I would like to ski more so I can be more confident. I would enjoy taking a class so I could look like those skiers on TV ads for ski resorts. I would also like to read a book with tips."

— *Amanda, age 23 from Colorado*

Four years ago, a reader of my weekly ski column approached me at a social gathering. "I admire you so much because you ski," she said.

Puzzled, I asked if *she* skied.

This Colorado native admitted she wanted nothing more than to be a skier. But unpleasant experiences on the slopes — and years of trying — had killed her enthusiasm. She felt guilty that she couldn't live up to the image of her home state.

Her testimony started me thinking about the conflicting attitudes women hold toward alpine skiing. Obviously, because I'm writing this book, I believe women hold a rightful place in the world of alpine skiing. But I've met so many women who have tried to ski and have been terribly frustrated — believing they're not strong enough, athletic enough, confident enough, to be good skiers.

So I began to research. I invited women friends and their friends to a focus group. I designed a survey and distributed it to women skiers wherever I found them. I cornered women on tennis courts, in gyms, parking lots and grocery stores, at Christmas parties and summer picnics. I invaded ski vacations of women from all over the world. I talked to day trippers and ski-town locals. I asked questions in lift lines, lunch lines, hot tubs, johns. On airplanes, shuttle buses, chair lifts and trams. At ski schools and preschools.

In the industry, I talked to instructors, educators, patrollers, racers, manufacturers, inventors, retailers and wholesalers, ski tuners and bootfitters. Fitness experts, physicians, physical therapists, psychologists and even a biomechanical engineer got visits from me.

To my amazement, women poured out their ski experiences. Their stories form the premise for this book: When it comes to recreational alpine skiing, many women are uninformed, unfit, and unnerved!

Believe it or not, I think that much of their alpine angst is caused by the ski industry itself. Since the rise in popularity of skiing with the end of World War II, women have been forced to use equipment designed for men and expected to perform on the slopes with the same reckless abandon as men.

Unable to do either, many women get complacent and settle in the intermediates' rut. They become experts at negative self-talk but secretly wish for more confidence and less fear. Women will stand frozen atop a steep mogul field, their mates and male friends yelling, "Ski down the fall line," and then blame themselves because they can't.

Before we examine why, let's look at another fact: Women are skiing more but enjoying it less.

The National Skier Opinion Survey of 21,500 skiers in the 1993/94 season shows that women comprised fewer than half of all skiers — 42.8 percent, down from 46.2 the previous year but still more than the 41.6 percent reported a few years earlier. That's the good news.

The bad news: Even though women comprised 54 percent of first-time skiers in 1993/94 (down from 62.4 percent in 1992/93), women tend to *stop skiing after only two years,* according to Jim Spring, president of the Boulder, Colorado-based research company.

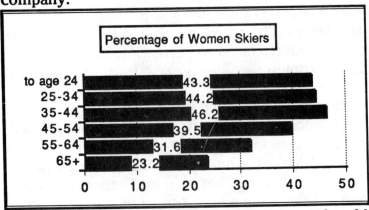

The truth: *Many women who can't get comfortable on the slopes would rather just quit.*

People in the U.S. ski industry would like to know why. They want the potential business these women represent. To get it, a few industry leaders are beginning to pay attention to women as skiers.

At last, ski-clothing and equipment manufacturers are acknowledging, just like disposable diaper makers did, that male and female bodies are different!

The idea that women skiers bring different needs to the sport is viable enough to warrant the formation of the first national Women's Education College of the Professional Ski Instructors of America (PSIA). Its founder, Beaver Creek ski instructor Carol Levine, also serves as a PSIA Rocky Mountain Division clinic leader and examiner and was selected to the prestigious (and mostly male) PSIA Demo Team.

The focus of the inaugural meetings in 1993 was understanding anatomical differences between men and women and their impact on skiing performance. Long-term goals include providing suggestions for teaching women based on physiological, psychological, and social influences in skiing. While the mechanics of skiing are the same for both sexes, their *attitudes* about the sport are vastly different.

"Women like a more stylish approach to skiing rather than the kamikaze approach," says Annie Vareille Savath, director of the ski school at Telluride Ski Resort and a pioneering founder of ski programs taught for women by women.

Indeed, wanting to perfect technique and look smooth and graceful were mentioned most as a skiing ideal in my survey of more than 300 women. But the style, beauty and grace of skiing have been overshadowed by machismo: Push the envelope, skate on thin ice, ski on the edge. This is how skiing is perceived today.

No wonder many women are saying, "Thanks," and then, "No thanks!" to skiing.

Now is the time for a book on alpine skiing that encourages women to embrace this sport and *enjoy* it as much as their mates, sons, fathers, brothers and friends. Recognizing the physical and mental uniqueness of women, this book presents evidence that *there are forces against women that may have more to do with inhibiting their skiing than lack of ability or courage.* In this book, I'll teach you to break barriers that prevent you from achieving your best and show you how skiing can be more *fun*, *safer*, and more *satisfying*. First-hand testimony from other women skiers will inspire you. Discussions on confidence will motivate you. Lessons in fear and injury prevention will calm you.

You'll learn to enjoy your days in the sun and on the snow by choosing and using the right equipment, clothing and accessories, and taking measures to stay healthy on the slopes. Top female instructors will teach you to ski in control — the No. 1 concern expressed by women and the key to skiing with confidence. They also offer tips on skiing moguls, steeps and gates as well as powder and ice.

You'll learn why women-teaching-women classes provide a learning atmosphere that breeds success. And you can choose a women's ski clinic that's right for you from a list of North American ski areas offering these programs.

I wrote this book for women skiers — beginners, experts, dropouts, terminal intermediates and, especially, wives whose husbands ask them to take a long lunch so they can do some *real* skiing. Men, too, should read this book to gain insight into the frustration women experience on the slopes and learn to encourage them.

My intention is not to bash male skiers or ski instructors. And I'm not suggesting women shouldn't ski with men. My purpose is to bridge the gender gap by showing women that they can ski on a par with men — or better!

Only when women learn all they can about their skiing will the industry take us seriously. If we show that we're ready to be players instead of cheerleaders, if we demand equipment that will enhance our performances, if we prove that technique, not brute force, makes a strong skier, we will profoundly change the rules of this sport.

I, for one, want to see the dreams of a 13-year-old Nebraska girl fulfilled: "I wish my body would be smooth and graceful coming down the hill," she wrote in my survey. "I wish that someday the curls would stay in my hair in cold weather. I hope someday I'll be the very best skier I can be."

How to read this book

Each chapter deals with a specific topic. To get the full flavor of the book, I suggest you read the chapters in order the first time, especially the first three. After that, refer to sections for information as you need it. For example, bootfitting is covered in Chapter Five, which deals with buying equipment; clothing is discussed in Chapter Ten, which tells you how to stay warm.

My goal for this book, more than anything, is to share what I've learned in 30-something years of skiing. I've monoboarded, snowboarded, heli-skied, snowcat-skied and snowskated at most major resorts in the United States and some in Europe.

I'm not a psychologist. I'm not a ski instructor. I am what you could call a clinic junkie. I have a backpack full of valuable tips from my years of attending clinics and taking lessons, as well as from my own considerable trials and errors.

I've been frustrated up there on the slopes. I've been scared and cold and I've fallen flat on my fanny in front of long lift lines. I've broken bones and pulled knee ligaments and even slammed into a tree. I skied through five pregnancies and left my own skiing on the back burner for years while my children learned. Now, as I pass along the joys of skiing to a new generation of skiers in the family, I *still* work on my technique.

I want to share with you the tricks that have gotten me here. My work as a ski journalist has provided me opportunities to learn industry secrets that will surprise you and help you.

Everything I've come to know continues to help me ski better. With each little improvement, I enjoy skiing more than I ever thought possible. Let me know if these tips help you, too. And, if you've discovered some secrets you'd like to share with other women, let's get a dialogue going. Together, we can change the climate for women in skiing from cool to HOT!

Write to me: PO Box 260061, Littleton, CO, 80126.
Have fun reading and **keep skiing!**

Claudia

Chapter One

Girls just want to have fun

"Men and women have totally different views on skiing. Men want to get to the bottom as fast as possible, whereas women want to improve their technical skills."

— *Glynis, age 47 from England*

"To be the skier I want to be, I need a personality change. Then I would be one of those skiers who goes straight down and never hesitates or traverses looking for an easier way."

— *Anne, age 29 from Colorado*

S everal times a year, Mary accompanies her husband, Jim, on ski trips to Vail. Every December, Jim participates in Pepi's Wedel Weeks, a week-long coed ski clinic, to get primed for the upcoming season. Meanwhile, Mary patiently practices her turns alone on the bunny hill at Beaver Creek, 10 miles west. Jim buys new equipment every year. Mary accepts hand-me-downs from her daughter. Jim shows marked improvement with each lesson, becoming powder proficient in Vail's back bowls. Mary plods along on the green slopes, never venturing from familiar terrain because she's afraid of going too fast and skiing out of control. She says she's "not good enough" to join the clinic. Jim calls his ski day "fantastic." Mary calls hers "terrifying."

The worst part of this scenario: Deep down, Mary *wants* to ski freely and fearlessly with her husband. She yearns to be part of what appears to her as a secret society of skiers. Heck, she just wants to have *fun*! But Mary has succumbed to the belief that she can't. Kept in the dark, she thinks she has no choice but to accept her second-class status or give up completely, as many women do.

Author Clarissa Pinkola Estés, in her best-selling book *"Women Who Run With the Wolves,"* (Ballantine Books, $23) reminds us that we all carry a taste of the Wild Woman within us ... "wild" meaning not out of control but the natural life force in all women.

She writes: "The memory is of our undeniable and irrevocable kinship with the wild feminine ... buried by overdomestication ... or no longer understood. ... Without her, women are silent when in fact they are on fire."

Women are expected to approach skiing with the same bravado and go-for-it attitude that their male counterparts bring to it. Some women can. But the majority, confused and uneasy with such expectations, feel faltering, even foreign, in the skiing world. When women need her most, their Wild Woman escapes them.

I encountered my Wild Woman as a high-school student, one winter afternoon in 1956 in my native Colorado. A fledgling on the bunny slope, I was nesting in the warming house at Winter Park with friends from the Eskimo Ski Club. Just as I was beginning to doubt I'd ever really ski, Josephine burst onto the scene, like a movie star greeting her fans.

Unquestionably the prettiest and most popular girl in the freshman class, Jo skied so much better than any of the girls that boys *allowed* her to ski with them all the time. Later that afternoon, as Jo and the boys approached our table, she brushed snow from her hair with a dramatic sweep of her hand and announced, "It's snowing *up top.*"

Up top. Those words became a metaphor for what I seek to this day every time I ski — the melding of mind and body, the elegance when it all comes together, the soothing of my soul in the beauty of winter. My Wild Woman compels me to go up top, to look for peaks beyond, to aspire higher. And I've learned to do it *my way*.

For men only?

Masculine traits always have set the standard for skiing: power, innate toughness, brute strength, competitiveness, aggressiveness, and a downright cocky attitude about athleticism. Telling a woman she "skis like a man," is considered a compliment by both sexes; telling a male he skis like a girl is taken as an insult. A woman who skis well is admired; a man who skis well simply is living up to expectations.

One man from Pennsylvania expressed this arrogance in a letter published in *Powder* magazine. He said he thinks the new wide-bodied powder skis, like the short beginner skis of the past, have "ruined skiing ... making it possible for fat housewives and their wimpy, accountant husbands to wedge gracelessly into my lines ... Skiing was better when it was elitist and an adventure. Trying to make it a sport for everyone ruins it for everybody," he wrote.

Slap this man! Tell him that, just because he has entered the kingdom, he can't close the gate behind him. Skiing is not *just* about speed, catching air, jumping cliffs and venturing into the unknown. Skiing is wonderful, but it's not to die for.

There's more than one way to ski. The ultimate experience doesn't have to be a steep, fast, frightening run down back-bowl slopes. Some people experience exhilaration and satisfaction from a seamless sequence of perfectly carved arcs. Or a wintry waltz through fresh powder. Or smooth 'n' easy gliding on a brilliant crisp day.

You're not alone if you like to *caress*, rather than *attack*, the hill. You don't need to hide on intermediate slopes if you prefer to *flow*, rather than *bash*, through bumps. If you concentrate on skiing with *finesse* instead of *force*, it doesn't mean you're a wimp!

Study the skiing of women instructors. Like ballet dancers, their technical mastery produces graceful moves that make skiing a thing of beauty.

Ski technique requires coordination and balance, agility and flexibility, endurance and strength — none of which lie beyond a woman's capability. Given the same mechanical advantages that men enjoy in skiing, there is no reason women, too, can't own this sport!

Old boys' club

A chauvinistic attitude prevails among recreational skiers, but male dominance really shines in ski racing. Of the 38 top administrators of U.S. Skiing, the governing body that oversees U.S. ski racing, only two were women as of the 1993-1994 ski season. Out of about 40 coaches of all men's and women's U.S. ski teams, one lone woman serves as a coach of the disabled team.

"Ski racing is an old boys' club," says Deb LaMarche, former director of athletic development of the U.S. Ski Team. "The sad thing is there are some really talented women coaches, and the opportunities are just not there." LaMarche took action after the 1993-94 ski season and formed an association for women coaches with the goal of opening doors previously closed to women.

Ironically, U.S. and Canadian women racers have won four times more Olympic and World Championship alpine medals than men! This proves the point. *Skiing itself is not gender-based, only attitudes make it so.*

Gender differences

Let's look at the psychological differences between men and women and how they apply to skiing. Psychologist John Gray, in his book, *"Men Are from Mars, Women Are from Venus"* (HarperCollins, $23), says a man's sense of self is defined by the ability to achieve results. "Martians [men] value power, competency, efficiency, and achievement," Gray writes. "They are always doing things to prove themselves and develop their power and skills.

"Instead of being goal oriented, women experience fulfillment through sharing and relating. They value love, communication, beauty, and relationships," he writes. "Involved in personal growth, they spend a lot of time supporting, helping, and nurturing one another."

How do these differences show up in skiing? Instructors will tell you that in ski classes, men want to learn a maneuver and go right on to the next — moving quickly toward that goal. They often misinterpret power for skill, using strength to turn instead of technique. They ski aggressively and physically.

Men love competition. A perfect example: One afternoon, I found myself the only woman skiing with four guys. After three lengthy bump runs, the guys decided they'd had enough of the technical stuff. Success in bump skiing is measured subjectively. They wanted — no, *needed* — a more goal-oriented challenge. They needed a contest. They chose a long, smooth course for our next run, then set the rules: Only three turns allowed. It reminded me of hearing as a kid, "The first one down, wins." Wins what? The right to boast about it of course.

Being the first one down and the last to leave the mountain earn bragging rights among men, but mean little to most women.

Women prefer doing it right and being in control over taking risks and chancing a fall. Women *must* develop good technique to ski well because they simply don't possess the physical strength required to muscle a turn. They enjoy skiing *with* friends, not *for* them. The tremendous success of women-only ski clinics confirms their supporting and nurturing qualities. Attempts at male-only clinics bomb. "Most men consider seeking help a weakness when they can solve a problem themselves," Gray says. If it's not broken, their instincts tell them to leave it alone.

One woman I met skiing told me she thinks men always are trying to prove something. "When I ski with my husband, I have better technique, look better, and I'm more in control," she says, "but he always thinks he has to be faster and better. Maybe it's just part of being a man."

She adds: "Men risk more. Women have more brains when it comes to safety. We know, if we hurt ourselves skiing, it won't be easy to take care of the house and the kids. But men have secretaries to help at the office and their wives to take care of them at home."

Another woman said when she surpassed her husband, who started skiing at the same time, he lost interest. "It was a real problem for him," she said. "Not only could I ski better, but I could also ski faster. Males are determined not to let you get ahead of them."

Here's what my survey participants said they notice about these male-female differences:

• Ego, a 23-year-old Japanese woman, says, "My brother likes to go fast and get air. I try to put more style and grace into my skiing instead of just going fast and out of control."

• Shelley, 50, from England, says the men she skis with like challenges. "I don't," she says. "I enjoy skiing where I *can* ski; they make an effort to ski where they don't think they can."

- Coloradan Patricia, 47, says, "I ski with more control and without a desire to go as fast and do as many runs as possible in a day. But I can keep up with them when I want to!"

- "Men like going full out, straight down," says Katie, 23, from England. "I'd rather go down trying to get style and rhythm, rather than going top to bottom without stopping."

- Twenty-seven-year-old Mindy, from Ohio, notices men ski beyond their ability. "Like in corporate America, they just go for it, whether they're going to get themselves killed or not!" she says. "I tend to ski within my ability and stretch my limits in increments."

- Madlyn, 52, from Michigan, says she dislikes the "pressure to achieve a higher level of skiing," which holds such importance with men.

- Andrea, 33, from Mexico City, thinks her husband "looks more secure" when he skis.

Forty-six-year-old Margaret, from Australia, told me about the time she skied a run with her son. At the bottom, he said, "Mom, there were some great jumps on that trail!"

"Really? She replied. "I didn't see one."

They went back and did it again. The run turned out to be infested with moguls. Margaret's son had taken them as opportunities to catch air while she had seen them as obstacles to ski around!

Like father, like son

To understand how gender differences in skiing are reinforced, let's peek at a typical children's ski-school scenario: Brother-and-sister Sally and

Sammy enter the children's center with mom and dad on the first day of the family ski vacation. Turning them over to an instructor, Dad lands a gentle punch on Sammy's shoulder: "Go get 'em, Tiger. Tear up that mountain, buddy boy!"

When Mom shows apprehension, Dad admonishes, "Leave him alone; he'll be fine." A high-five with Dad and Sammy's off with a clear message.

To his daughter, Dad warns: "Be careful, princess."

Mom and Dad bend down to give Sally hugs and kisses.

"Bye, bye, sweetheart," Dad says.

"If you get cold, be sure to come in," Mom adds.

On some days Sammy goes to class alone because Sally goes shopping with mom. It's acceptable for girls to take a day or two off but the men need to rack up that manly vertical.

Twenty years later, Sam meets a friend at the top of a double-black-diamond run.

"Hey, big guy, how's it going?"

Sam answers, "I'm *tearing* up the mountain, man. Just jumped off that cliff. I was outta control but pulled it out. Wanna do this run, Dude? Last one down buys the beer.

"Go get 'em, Tiger," Sam says, punching "Tiger" on his arm. Sam spits and pushes off, straight down the middle.

Meanwhile, Sally skis carefully on the green slopes. She'd love to ski with her husband but won't move to more difficult runs because she fears getting hurt.

"My feet are killing me and my hands are numb," Sally confides to friends over a hot-chocolate break. "And some kid almost ran into me with his snowboard. I think I'll quit early and go shopping."

A supervisor of children (age 6-12) at Golden Peak Children's Center in Vail, Todd Williams notices a strong cultural emphasis for boys to be strong and girls to be protected, even in skiing. Around age 7, boys begin to get aggressive on the slopes. Williams says: "They don't worry about speed. They just go straight down, whereas girls want control.

"Girls also demonstrate more concern for their friends in the classes than do boys. When we switch the kids to different classes, girls get very upset because they don't want to leave their friends," Williams says. "But boys don't care."

I saw the same in my own five children, all of whom started skiing at age 4. My two girls were "pretty" skiers. They loved to bring their friends, meander along favorite trails and take long hot-chocolate breaks.

My three boys constantly were darting into the trees, then shooting out on the trails. They skied steep moguls the same as flat, groomed runs — straight down. Never satisfied to just ski, they either raced each other or were flying off jumps. In the 1970s, my young sons copied the back-flips of the hot-doggers of the day, many of whom landed in the hospital with broken backs. The boys assured me they weren't flipping, but I knew.

Williams notices fathers pushing their sons in skiing. When boys are placed in a slow group, often dads come unglued and demand a stronger ability level, but when this happens to daughters, dads don't complain as much.

Gracie Goodwin, the manager of the Vail children's center, says she's noticed that girls who grow up in ski towns ski more on a par with boys.

"Skiing on Vail Mountain is like the swing set in their backyard," Goodwin says. "Girls here grow up athletically feminine."

Athletically feminine. These words pack a powerful punch for those who want a woman "to ski like a man." Sports like gymnastics, ice skating, horseback riding, even tennis, allow women to express themselves in an athletically feminine way. Yet in skiing, women are expected to perform *athletically masculine!*

I believe this is why most women hold themselves in such low regard as skiers. In the National Skier Opinion Survey, 75 percent more women than men said they would ski more often if only they could ski better! In my survey, women said they need to beef up their courage, self-confidence and aggressiveness in order to ski as well as they'd like.

Let's explore how to do this. Because more courage and less fear rank high on the list, I've devoted Chapter Nine to fear. We'll examine self-confidence and aggressiveness here.

Self-confidence

Self-confidence is acquired, not inherited. So says Judith Briles in her book, *"The Confidence Factor"* (MasterMedia Ltd., $12.95), based on *The Keri® Report: Confidence and the American Woman,* a nationwide survey of 6,000 people. The 1990 book explores why women lack self-confidence and prescribes a list of Ten Commandments to improve self-image and enhance self-respect.

The Keri Report suggests that confidence "comes to women through their risk taking, crises, even failures, and their ability to bounce back from these events," Briles writes. "Confidence is strengthened by difficulties — not rose gardens."

My experience has shown me that this is indeed true: Confidence in skiing is acquired by overcoming challenges — striving to be comfortable on one skill level, then moving on to the next. Women with no physiological barriers (we'll discuss that in Chapters Two and Three) *can* build confidence steadily as they add new skills and advance to more difficult terrain and snow.

First, let's look at women who possess self-confidence in spades, and learn what motivates them.

Nurturing self-esteem

In skiing, no one encounters more challenges than members of the ski patrol. At Jackson Hole, one of the United States' steepest, toughest skiing mountains, five of its 47 patrollers are women.

Their job starts before dawn when they ready the mountain for skiing. It's pitch black and bitter cold. While you and I sleep, these women ride to the top of the mountain where, in snow past their knees, they throw bombs to force slides down any of 142 avalanche-prone spots. When they're not bombing, the women haul crates of explosives, shovel snow and debris, set up poles, fencing and signs, remove rocks from runs — all before the lifts open.

During the day, they respond to calls from injured skiers, administer first aid, check barricades, and police runs for reckless or out-of-control skiers and powder hounds slipping out of bounds. When the sun begins to set, the women help sweep the mountain for stranded skiers.

The scariest part of this job is "ski checking." In this snow-control procedure, patrollers monitor each other's solo crossings of snow fields, zig-zagging one by one, often in front of ominous cliffs that could thunder into avalanches at any moment. As they watch each other, the thought is always there: Can I move fast enough to save a life if the mountainside lets loose?

Each of these women acknowledges the influence of strong support from their mothers, which they believe helps to account for their positive self-perception. Each demonstrates a willingness to accept hard work and meet challenges. All share a love of skiing and the outdoors. The greatest satisfaction of the job is knowing they can do it.

"I need to prove to myself that I can do it," says Suzanne Hagerman, who admits to being timid and afraid of heights as a young girl. "But I've always been strong-willed. That's what keeps me going."

Cindy Budge, told 20 years ago at a Utah resort that girls didn't do well on the ski patrol, says: "This job has taught me what I'm capable of. You don't have to be a pretty skier to patrol, just strong.

You have to be able to ski down anything pulling a rig. You need to know the mountain, have mountaineering skills and first-aid training. We feel strong, although the mountain is always humbling."

Though they perform difficult and dangerous tasks, these women are not superhuman. They are mothers, wives, sisters, friends. Off season, they sew, garden, waitress, work in retail sales. *They are no different from you and me except they believe in their ability to handle the consequences of risks they take.* Though their physical strength might not equal a man's, the intensity these women bring to their work makes up for it.

Confidence in competition

Deb LaMarche, who has worked for 20 years with U.S. Ski Team athletes, says women racers exhibit a similar mental toughness.

"There's a certain drive to be the best they can be," LaMarche says. "A lot come from families where daughters are considered important and as having as much potential as sons; where parents think daughters can do anything." Consequently, they excel at everything they do. The majority are also honor-roll students, she adds.

Patti Sherman, a two-time champion of the Women's Pro Mogul tour, found her family's support an important ingredient of her self-confidence and skiing success. "My family pushed us to do sports — not necessarily to win, but to build confidence and believe in ourselves," Sherman says. "I never compared myself to other women. I compared myself to whomever was out there. I didn't care if I was the best little girl. I just wanted to be as good as my big brother. Mentally, you've got to believe deep inside you can do it."

Speed skier Amy Guras, clocked at 126 mph on skis in 1993, agrees that mental conditioning is the key to confidence. "The fun in speed skiing is to go beyond what you've ever done," Guras says. "You've got to let your mind *think* your body has the ability. I think I can ski better than I can walk down stairs!"

Guras, 32, who owns The Racer's Edge ski shop in Breckenridge with husband, Greg (also her technician) was one of only 30 women to clock their speed on a 20-second-long, straight, steep course in Les Arcs, France, where speed skiing debuted as a demonstration sport at the 1992 Olympic Games.

Passing on the kind of parental support she received when she started skiing at age 3, Guras encourages her 5-year-old daughter, Alexandra, to do whatever she wants.

"Kids have no fear ... I'm not going to hold her back," Guras says. "When we're hiking, if she sees a big boulder, I'll say, 'Go climb it.'" Alexandra, who skis straight down in a tuck, says, "I like to go fast — just like you, Mommy!"

Kristen Ulmer is one of a handful of women gutsy enough, and crazy enough, to enter and win extreme skiing competitions on the gnarliest, nastiest mountains in the world. Ulmer says in an article she authored for *Skiing* magazine that it helps to be born with an invincible attitude you can build on.

"It takes the finest genetic makeup and years of scraping by to become an ass-kicking skier," Ulmer wrote. Also essential, she said, is a huge ego and a "superhero" attitude. "With each new successful descent, cliff jump, or stunt, that feeling becomes stronger," the extreme queen wrote. "After a horrible [but] injury-free crash, you feel like King of the Hill because you got away with it. You've always gotten away with it!"

Ulmer, star of numerous ski movies, shares her secrets in the annual Women's Ski Clinic at Hidden Valley, N.J. (See Chapter 13.)

Confidence knows no age boundaries. Eighty-year-old Colorado ski pioneer Edna Dercum still dons her helmet every season to compete in the downhill on the national and international Masters ski-race circuit. In 1993, Dercum added another gold medal to the hundreds of trophies spanning a racing career that began in 1938.

Dercum, who once built and ran a ski lodge with her husband, Max — a founder of Arapahoe Basin and Keystone ski areas — says the key to confidence is "learning good, controlled skiing." She also believes skiing confidence is fostered by parental involvement: "Skiing was a bond that kept us close [with two children]. Skiing has made our grandchildren more gutsy, more eager to try other things."

When Dercum hears about women giving up skiing because they think they're too old, she says she'd like to have introduced them to her mother-in-law, who took up alpine skiing at 65. At 90, she decided to switch to cross-country because it was less demanding! She skied cross-country until age 98, and then lived to 104!

For every "ass-kicking" woman skier out there, hundreds more are just looking for the nerve to point 'em a little straighter down the fall-line.

To find out how to get it, let's apply Briles' "Ten Commandments of Confidence" to skiing:

I. To your own self be true.

Ski for thee! Kara Makata , a Winter Park ski instructor, says women often enroll in lessons because someone asks them to. "They hate it!" Makata says. "They're frightened. They don't want to be there."

Breckenridge instructor Jan Degerberg encourages women not to allow their husbands to make decisions about lessons for them. "And when you state your goals to the instructor, make them *your* goals," Degerberg says. "Remember, this is *your* experience!"

Annie Black, a Keystone instructor, has seen enough of "analysis paralysis" in her 20 years of teaching skiing. "Sometimes men try too hard to get us to ski by tearing our skiing apart," she says. "Women should ski for their own sense of accomplishment," Black says, instead of trying to "get better than someone else," as men often want them to do.

Black believes going fast does not measure success in skiing. She warns women not to set themselves up for failure by skiing faster than their comfort level allows. "Set a rule for yourself: You never need to go faster than you want," Black advises. "Skiing is supposed to be fun. If your husband or friend won't ski with you because you're too slow, find someone else to ski with." If speed is not your bag, reinforce other strengths and concentrate on them. Technical skills like running gates and skiing powder make a strong skier.

My friend Barbara says she's happiest skiing with people who ski at her level. "I could ski just Northwoods at Vail all day and love it," Barbara says. "Then, we'll meet someone on the mountain and they want to ski something over my head. So, I go along. Then I get perched on the top of something I can't ski and I can't move. I lose my form and my confidence, and I start skiing uphill to control my speed instead of down."

"When you're planning your ski group, try to include at least one other person of your skill level," Black suggests. This way, if the pressure to go faster or ski a run that's too difficult becomes debilitating, you can hang back with each other.

Dorcas, 49, from Pennsylvania, has it figured out: "When I first started skiing, I always asked, 'How did I look?'" she says. "Now I realize I ski for my recreation, and if I enjoyed my run, I don't care how it looked to someone else. I ski for fun and I don't feel my skill level limits that enjoyment."

Wild Woman!

II. Create positive thinking

I witnessed a classic example of negative self-talk when I skied in a blizzard with two women friends. One saw the deepening snow as a rare opportunity to practice her emerging powder skills. The other woman, a competent enough skier, was not a happy camper. Though she was making nice, round, even turns and not falling, she kept protesting that she was out of her element. But by telling herself she couldn't ski powder and then retreating to the lodge, she missed the chance to continue learning.

Winter Park instructor Mary Moynihan says women should think about "tactical self-talk."

"Women know negative self-talk is not productive and they don't really *believe* positive self-talk," Moynihan says. By telling yourself you can do something, you're setting yourself up to answer, "No, I can't!" So, Moynihan suggests talking to yourself about ski *tactics* — things like keeping your hands up or your shoulders square to the fall line. This take-charge self-talk gets your mind off the confidence issue and focuses on the skiing.

"It's an attitude," says Shelley Scipione, a 22-year-old girls' ski coach from Vermont. "You just have to say, 'I'm going to do it.' When I was learning to do a helicopter [360-degree turn in midair], I thought, 'Ooh, this is scary!' I did it halfway the first time, all the way the next," Scipione recalls. "Now, every time I do one, it's still kind of scary. But I just say to myself, 'People don't die doing this. If somebody else can do it, why can't I?'"

When people get into a mind-set that says, "I can't," it keeps them stuck, says Denver psychotherapist Mimi Kaplish. They get the idea they are powerless and not in control or able to make changes. "Words can change this attitude," Kaplish says. "Next time someone wants you to ski where you know you'll be in trouble, instead of saying, 'I can't,' use the words, 'I don't choose to.'

"This is a very empowering phrase," Kaplish says. "It means 'I have choices, and for whatever reason, I access my ability to make a choice and this is it.'" This leaves the path open to try another time.

Another phrase that undermines power is the negative "I-should" phrase. "This implies authority outside myself telling me what is right for me," Kaplish says. Once again, you become a powerless victim instead of an empowered person.

III. You are not alone.

Trust me. Confidence is an issue with women — in skiing and in life! For example, in a 1993 survey of 151 women published in *First for Women*, 51 percent admitted that more self-confidence would make them happier about their self-image.

In my survey, self-confidence ranks second after technique as the answer to my question: "What is one thing in your skiing you would like to change or improve?"

Of the 300 women who filled out my written survey, plus hundreds more with whom I talked, responses show that many, mostly beginners and intermediates, feel a lack of confidence on the slopes. Even some instructors and self-described experts in my survey said they would like to feel more comfortable on difficult snow and terrain.

Again and again, I read admissions like this: "I really need more confidence in myself so I can grow in my abilities and evolve past this plateau

I've reached." If you think this way, you are not alone.

IV. Learn something new.

Mastering something — anything — builds confidence in any stage of life. Consider toddlers: After their first step, if they didn't have confidence to take another, then another, they would never learn to walk. Sports, especially individual sports like skiing, offer great opportunities for building confidence because the learning curve involves setting and meeting small, doable, measurable goals. With each goal mastered, you gain confidence to move forward and learn something new. Pretty soon, you've moved through the whole process and it becomes a matter of fine tuning.

Don't take too big a leap at one time. You'll set yourself up for disappointment. Anne, 40-ish, admits, "The one thing I would like to improve is my confidence level — it's hard to try new things when you're afraid. I need to build up confidence slowly."

Take lessons to learn new techniques. Learning to ski correctly in the beginning proves far better than trying to change bad habits later on that will hold you back. When you get stuck, you lose not only the ability to progress, but confidence, too. You need to keep learning!

V. Assess the situation.

Women know how to do this well. They meticulously check out trails before they try them, approach difficult runs prudently, and ski cautiously on unfamiliar terrain. Ask any man and he'll tell you women react *too* cautiously. Timid is used by a lot of men to describe women skiers. But they don't understand: We are *assessing* the situation!

So what about off the mountain? A reality check of your life can help you understand why skiing may be a source of diminishing self-confidence and frustration. A relationship with a controlling man, for instance, can cause lack of self-esteem. This will surely carry over to the slopes.

Responsibility for small children or aging parents, demanding jobs, extensive travel or any circumstance beyond our control can squelch the best of wintertime getaway plans. If you're in a lean ski year, don't beat yourself up when you finally do get up skiing because you find your confidence has eroded.

Put it in perspective: Understand that one important factor in gaining assurance in skiing is mileage. When you build up vertical miles, you'll build up confidence.

VI. Give yourself credit for your accomplishments.

We all know praise generates self-esteem. Yet women hesitate making a big deal about little achievements in skiing. Men, however, find no such problem. For some, exchanging ski stories over beers at the end of the day can be as fulfilling as the actual feats.

A few years ago we visited my oldest daughter, Susan, when she was living in Utah. She's a high-energy, self-confident, do-it-all kind of woman. We coaxed her from a busy schedule to ski with us at Snowbird for a day. After she breezed down The Cirque (a huge bowl scooped out of a steep mountainside), we laughed about her chalking up yet another accomplishment. She had just become a mother, gotten a job, bought a new house ... *and* she skied The Cirque! Though we joke about it even now, I know it remains a source of pride.

Women like and need pats on the back, says ski instructor Annie Black. "If you can't get them from your husband or boyfriend, learn to give them to yourself."

VII. *Aspire higher.*

Diann Roffe-Steinrotter, who captured gold for the United States in Super-G at the 1994 Olympics, credits her career wins, including a 1985 World Championship, with striving to get better.

"At my first Olympics in '88, I realized that I was really good, that I was a woman, and that there aren't that many opportunities for women in sports," Roffe-Steinrotter says. "I knew people would kill to be in my shoes — to be an Olympian — and I was just kind of going through the motions. So I said I've got to settle down, get stronger, more concentrated. I gritted my teeth and said, 'OK, I'm going to get better at this.'"

A slow building process ensued. "I just worked on my confidence, year after year, day after day. I did everything I could to make it more difficult in training so the races would be easy. I tried to do everything right."

Roffe-Steinrotter won her first Olympic silver at Méribel, France in 1992 and retired a champ after Lillehammer in 1994.

"I had full confidence in all the work I'd done in my whole career," Roffe-Steinrotter says. "The minute I had any preconceived ideas of how good I was, I stunk! So I tried to stay humble and work on what I had to do to ski fast."

Her advice to women: Be realistic about your ability ... then gradually inch away at getting better. Your confidence will build and you won't even know it.

VIII. Get some feedback.

Women-only clinics offer great opportunities to women for skiing feedback. Constructive criticism delivered in a gentle, non-threatening manner by understanding women instructors proves a powerful tool in ski teaching and confidence-building. (In Chapter Thirteen, I discuss women's ski seminars and list U.S. ski areas with such programs.)

Often, women don't get the encouragement and support they need from husbands, boyfriends or family. One man said to me: "Sure, I *let* my wife go skiing. But I always tell her when she walks out the door that if she breaks a leg, she'll still have to take care of the kids and drive them to school every morning."

Imagine this woman skiing all day with that message playing in her head: Don't break a leg! I can't believe she has much fun, or that she will advance.

During the 1994 Olympics, it wasn't hard to figure out why a Russian cross-country skier told *USA Today* that she didn't want to phone home. "Every time I call, my husband tells me to come back," she told the newspaper. "He's getting impatient." Knowing what he was impatient for, she added, "I don't *like* cooking. I'd rather go eat at my mom's place."

IX. Take care of yourself.

In upcoming chapters, we'll talk about taking care of equipment: your body and your ski gear. Now, let's talk about the care and feeding of your psyche, also an important part of ski accoutrements.

On ski vacations, most women bear the responsibility of the children, described in my survey as one of the "hassles" of skiing. According to the National Skier Opinion Survey, more women ski with children (62 percent) than do men (53 percent), and married men with children are more likely to ski with their buddies than with their families.

Amy, a friend of mine, recalls: "It was always my responsibility to ski with the children. My husband would meet us for lunch and maybe take one run with us. Once the children got better than I was, they went off on their own. It got pretty lonely skiing by myself." She's come close to quitting many times.

Let *him* ski with the children sometimes! Or, ski together as a family. But don't make yourself sole caretaker on the slopes.

Treat yourself to some expert coaching. Multi-day clinics can be fun mini-vacations, as well as great opportunities for breakthroughs in your skiing. Take lessons with your husband or boyfriend only if your relationship is supportive and non-competitive.

In an early-season clinic I attended at Copper Mountain, a husband and wife (psychologists who should have known better) showed the rest of us how not to find marital bliss on the slopes. He relentlessly berated her in class on her techniques, especially her tendency to ski with stiff legs. But he got his due when, during the group video critique, our instructor pointed out the very same mistakes in *his* skiing as the ones for which he was harassing his wife!

When my young friends Kent and Beth married in their early 20s, Kent's skiing ability far surpassed Beth's. He easily could have said, "See ya!" and skied off with the guys. But he says he figured spending a season to help and encourage Beth on the slopes might ensure lots of togetherness later on. Today, the couple telemark in the high country around their log cabin in Summit County, Colorado — a perfectly matched couple. (No, he doesn't have a brother.)

X. Keep in circulation.
- Ski as much as you can.
- Hang out with skiers; join a ski club.
- Buy a home or time-share condo at a ski resort if you're considering a second home.

- If you live close to a ski area, drive up regularly with friends or sign up for weekly bus trips. Or, start your own group and charter a bus.
- Take at least one ski vacation a year. Read *"Skiing America"* guidebook (World Leisure, $17.95) or *"Ski Europe"* (World Leisure, $16.95), both by Charles Leocha, for an annually-updated, insider's scoop on everything from ski schools to sushi in America and Europe's major resorts.
- Cut lift-ticket costs by using coupons and ski-discount cards and buying multiple-day tickets.
- Invest in a subscription to a ski magazine: *Snow Country*, *Ski*, *Skiing* and *Powder*. *Skiing for Women*, which debuted in 1994, has found an instant audience. Stay abreast of your hometown newspaper's ski coverage in sports and travel sections.

Aggressiveness

Ski instructors, usually males, constantly tell women to be more aggressive and let themselves get a little out of control. Society pulls us in the opposite direction. The notorious lady-in-the-parlor, whore-in-the-bedroom begs for attention, again.

Julie Woodworth Buniva, 30, a professional ski racer, says women need to step away from their submissive selves when they're on the slopes. "To reach the next level in skiing, you really need to be aggressive — not mean, just have more fight and feistiness," she says. But most women, especially those born before 1964, are as uncomfortable with the notion of getting aggressive in skiing as they would be robbing a bank. They cannot overcome years of socialization in two or three ski lessons, explains Denver psychologist Linda Lister.

"Aggressiveness may not fit with a woman's self-concept," Lister says. And those instructors and husbands who think they're helping when they tell women to "get aggressive" only intimidate them and make them feel worse about their skiing. It's just not a command a woman immediately can respond to, such as "turn your shoulders," or "bend your knees."

Try this instead: Set a goal, then work out a system for achieving it, says Lister. If you want to ski faster or straighter, just call it that. Don't psyche yourself out by calling it "getting aggressive."

"Just do it" — but do it in control

Becoming aggressive involves skill. Instructor Mary Moynihan remembers a student who struggled until she finally learned to ski in control. "Once she realized technique would control speed," Moynihan says, "she could do anything." Her confidence *and* aggressiveness improved dramatically. "That's the key," Moynihan says. "I don't think women are less aggressive, *they just need to be in control.*"

It all comes down to technique.

Alice, 53, from Connecticut, recalls skiing bumps at a resort in New England. She was linking perfect turns in the fall line, she says, when a man from the chair lift had the nerve to yell, "Go faster!" A woman on the same lift, enraged, yelled back, "She looks fabulous. Leave her alone!"

I've skied with Alice. I wouldn't describe her as aggressive, but she does ski bumps with precision and authority because she knows how to control her turns. That man on the lift should be so lucky!

Rock-a-bye-bye bumps

No matter how much aggressiveness you do bring to the slopes, don't be surprised if it goes on maternity leave once you become a mother. It's amazing how you instinctively take the edge off your skiing when you have the responsibility of children. Just about every skiing mother I know — instructors included — admits to toning down her risk-taking. Even men notice the taming effect of motherhood on the women around them.

Society doesn't regard hard-core skiing as part of motherhood and apple pie. I remember skiing with friends of my teenage son at Steamboat. Trying to build enough speed to propel myself over a knoll, I got in a downhill tuck. As I took off, I heard one of the boys say: "Wow! Mike's mom *tucks*!"

After Mike blew out both knees playing football in high school, I heard one of his buddies ask if he'd still be able to ski.

"Sure," Mike said. "I'll just have to ski like my mom."

Kay, another woman who took part in my survey, said she remembers being nervous on ski slopes when her children were little. "I could never relax because these big men would come down like they were crazy and I was afraid they'd hit my little kids," she says. A mom's peripheral vision gets a workout!

A mother can't separate herself, says Sharon, a Colorado skier. Recently, she was so preoccupied with helping her 7-year-old daughter get on the lift that she forgot to get on herself. The lift — and her daughter — went up without her! Interesting, isn't it, that she never worries about her 10-year-old son: "He skis in control and can stop on a dime," Sharon says.

If motherhood has curbed your assertiveness on the slopes, be patient. It'll come back.

I wouldn't trade skiing as a family for anything. Though I skied with much less boldness and attention to my own skiing when my children were little, I was able to witness them developing *their* skills and confidence. I knew the time would come when I'd be chasing their tails!

Push yourself — gently

I found practical, compassionate advice about "letting go" in skiing from Dave Merriam in a video featuring fellow P.S.I.A. Demo Team members, Dee Byrne and Nancy Oakes, teaching the art of carving turns. Merriam compares pushing yourself in skiing to balancing on a fence.

In this excerpt from the video, *"The Signature of Excellence"* (Driscoll Communications, $19.95), Merriam explains this balancing act:

> I call it the 'Risk Fence.' The better your skills, the wider the fence and the easier it is to balance on it.
>
> On one side of the fence is frustration — the area that represents the feeling of holding on, the time when you don't let go ... On the other side lurks catastrophe — the zone you may fall into if you push it too far ... if you don't have the skills or know your personal limits.

Walking on the fence is the essence of the sport. It's exhilarating: this is your peak performance. ... You might have to jump on the fence to grow as a skier. If risk-taking becomes necessary, do it intelligently:

- Know your abilities, the limits of your equipment and the condition of the slope.
- Be aware of how you respond to pressure; only then can you make good decisions.
- Be aware of your environment; don't focus inward.
- Choose uncrowded runs and those relatively easy for you.
- Ski the trail a few times so you know it well.
- As you gain comfort with a skill and decide to push it a little more, do it when you won't endanger anyone else.
- Be warmed up physically and mentally. Pay attention — don't let your mind wander.
- Quit when you're tired, or find less demanding terrain or snow.

To risk wisely, it's imperative you are aware of all elements and consequences of your actions. By taking *calculated risks*, you may find sources of strengths and finesse you never dreamed existed. By pushing yourself intelligently and stretching your abilities, you may find you come closer to reaching your potential as a skier.

Ski smart, ski safe, and ski in control.

In the remainder of this book, we'll learn to do exactly that.

Chapter Summary

Skiing has always been defined according to male standards. The pressure to "ski like a man" and be more aggressive causes many women to suppress how they really want to ski—smoothly and gracefully. Athletically feminine.

In this chapter we reviewed genetic differences between men and women and how social conditioning perpetuates these differences on the slopes.

You learned ways to build confidence in skiing. You also learned that internal motivation — rather than aggressiveness, which is external — is a more natural way for women to succeed in skiing. Aggressiveness may not fit with a woman's self-concept, and it tends to decrease with motherhood. There are other ways to ski with authority. Learning to ski in control is the key.

Lastly, extending your limits in skiing is like balancing on a fence. Dave Merriam shows how to push yourself wisely to reach your full potential.

Recommended viewing:

"The Signature of Excellence:" To order, write Driscoll Comm., P.O. Box 1197, Stowe, VT 05672, or call (800) 424-0033.

Chapter Two

Why can't a woman ski like a man?

"I've been skiing for 36 years and I never get any better. There must be a little trick I'm missing. My biggest problem is my knees get in the way."
— *Judy, age 56 from Colorado*

"I'm terribly disappointed [in my skiing] because I have always been athletic and been in all types of sports."
— *JoAnne, age 46 from California*

"My ex-husband would get very frustrated with me because what he'd suggest to improve didn't ooze right out of my body — especially my legs and feet."
— *Jane, age 41 from Colorado*

D on't be misled by this chapter's title. I am not suggesting women should ski like men. This title refers to the biomechanical obstacles that prevent many women from learning and progressing in skiing as readily as men.

When you're perched on the chair lift, it's easy to spot women on the slopes below. And it's not because they're wearing tight stretch pants or purple boots. It's because of their form — bent at the waist, butts out, knees together, skis splayed.

Why is it so much easier to pick out other women's flaws than to correct your own technique? And when you see a man skiing as though his skis are an extension of his feet, do you wonder if there's something he knows that you don't? And why, you also may wonder, are you skiing at the same level after all these years?

If you can't find the answers, you will be happy to know that lack of ability may not be what separates you from the skier you want to be. *You can blame it on your female body!*

The Q angle

The anatomical characteristic that makes our bodies ideal for having children — our pelvis, or hip bones — also creates problems for us on the ski slopes. The broad central cavity of the female pelvis is designed for carrying babies. At the lower part of this bony framework are ball-and-socket joints to which the thigh bone (femur) connects. These joints allow the legs to move in many directions and bear all the weight of the trunk and upper body. Because a woman's pelvis is wider than a man's, the points where the femurs attach are farther apart. And with the female femur also shorter, a pronounced "V" is created from the hips to the knees.

Now, if you draw two imaginary straight lines, one down the femur and the other up the tibia (large bone of the lower leg), the angle created by the intersection of those lines in the mid-patella region (knee) is what orthopedic doctors and physiologists call the "Q angle." (Fig. 1.) Q angle is medical shorthand for the angle of the *quadricep* tendon.

Why should we care about the Q angle?

Q angle

Figure 1

Any skier, male or female, must have good *balance*. In fact, in their book *"The Athletic Skier"* (The Athletic Skier, Inc., $24.95), ski teachers-authors David Evrard and Warren Witherell say good balance is not enough — it has to be *perfect:* "You must strive for perfect balance ... Imperfect balance inhibits performance." They stress, "No other issue is more important to your progress as a skier."

Perfect balance requires perfect alignment — this is the overall principle in ski instruction. "Proper alignment allows you to do anything you want on skis," says Annie Vereille Savath, Telluride's ski school director. "It makes you agile and quick," she says. "When you are out of alignment, you are not going to be ... technically correct."

Picture how the pole of a carousel pony passes through its center as it moves up and down in the same spot. We want to maintain an imaginary pole from the tops of our heads through our centers. Proper alignment continues that vertical line as *straight* as possible down the legs and over the ankles and feet.

But, thanks to the Q angle, this is not the normal skiing stance for many women. The wider the hips, the more crooked the legs.

If you have ever been told you run like a girl, this means you run with your lower legs kicking to the side, or knock-kneed — a position created by the Q angle. When you ski, this position (affectionately called The Virgin Clutch by ski instructors) creates an A-frame from your knees to your skis. All this body geometry — the A frame, the Q angle, the V femur — adds up to plain old bad alignment for skiing.

Cindy Suplizio, a biomechanical engineer, has long believed that an excessive Q angle can make skiing more difficult for women. "An increased Q angle at the knee joint results in *less than optimal alignment* of the femur and tibia," Suplizio says. While at the Steadman-Hawkins Sports Medicine Foundation in Vail, considered a foremost center of research and education in sports-medicine orthopedics, she embarked on a fact-finding mission to learn about the Q angle's effect on injuries among female skiers.

Remember Pipi Longstocking, the endearing children's literature character, with her braids sticking out and her knock knees above her rumpled socks? Pipi would have major problems trying to ski, not because of lack of ability, but because her knees don't line up over her feet. It's biomechanics. Pipi and the skiing sisterhood that grew up reading about her can't help it!

So what's a girl to do?

Not all women are cursed by a Q angle. And some are more "Q'd" than others. Take a look at the figure of your next female ski instructor. It's no coincidence that most top-ranked women skiers are built straight and narrow. Women with curvy bodies and pronounced Q angles usually don't make it to the highest levels of perfection in skiing. You're in luck if you have hips like a teenage boy's.

If you're not sure whether this applies to you and you haven't had much luck skiing, there's a good chance your Q angle could be part of your problem.

"If a woman has a very large Q angle, she's probably not going to enjoy skiing very much and will be more likely to quit," says Kacey Conway, a physical therapist and specialist in sports medicine. Conway spends a lot of time working as a ski guide in Colorado at Copper Mountain where she frequently encounters such women unable to perform basic maneuvers required to ski. "Excessive Q angle can be very self-limiting," Conway says.

Here's how to figure your Q angle:

• **Stand with your feet pointed forward, about six inches apart, in your normal parallel skiing stance.** Look straight ahead, then drop your knees as though you were pushing on your boot cuffs to initiate a turn.

• **Look straight down.** Do your knees touch, or at the very least, go in? Can you see one or both of your feet peeking to the outsides of your knees? If the center of your knee is not over your big toe you're not aligned correctly for skiing.

• **Try to edge, as if you were turning to the left.** It's difficult to get a strong edge set with your right foot, or downhill ski, because your left knee is pressed inward against your right knee!

• **Now, using your quad muscles, move your knees so they are centered over your toes.** Edge again in this position. See how much more easily you can roll to the sides of both feet, and how much farther you can lean on your edges? Imagine how dynamically you could ski with this extended range of movement.

• **Try this in front of a mirror.** Look at the angulation (comma position) you achieve. Bingo! This is the difference between slipping and edging, skidding and carving, intermediate and advanced skiing!

• **Now, try to edge as if you were turning to the right.** Like many women, you may have one knee that turns in more than the other. This could be the reason it's more difficult for you to turn this direction when you're on skis. (My easier-turning side, called "the chocolate side" by an instructor named Gabi, is not as Q'd. You probably have a chocolate side, too.)

Roll zee knees, pleeze

While the uphill edge is mostly unweighted (some racers lift that ski completely off the snow), you still want your knees pointing in the same direction. Telluride instructor Melissa Eddlestein says the knees should chase but never catch each other when you're in the skiing stance. Picture how a team of horses looks pulling a sleigh. The horses don't touch, but they trot alongside each other; in a turn, the inside horse is slightly ahead.

When he's teaching advanced ski clinics, extreme skier Eric DesLauriers demonstrates the proper position for the knees by placing his hands as if in prayer and sliding them between his knees. "Skiing is basically rolling your knees from side to side like this," he tells his students.

It's a simple enough premise. Everyone can roll their knees just so, right? But remove the hands from between the knees and, if you're a woman, your knees naturally want to greet each other like long-lost buddies. Men's knees, on the other hand, will hold in the correct position.

How many times have you heard your husband or your boyfriend or your son or your male ski instructor tell you to *drive* your knees into the turn, or pretend your knees are headlights, or *steer* with your knees? This is easy for them because their hips, knees and feet line up in the same vertical plane. When men "bend zee knees," zee knees usually bend right over their boots, which transmits the action to the ski. (Assuming they're wearing properly fitting ski boots. We'll talk about the art of bootfitting in Chapters Four and Five.)

Men who try to help us improve our skiing don't understand why we can't "Just turn!" Or "Ski straighter down the fall line!" Or "Go faster!" Granted, sometimes it's fear, but it's also because *our feet don't move like men's.* Feet are not as quick to respond to knees that hug all the way down the hill.

Ride a flat ski

The starting point in skiing begins with both boots flat on the skis, skis flat on the snow. Your boot must be completely flat on the ski and your foot in a neutral position in the boot for you to roll your ski effectively from edge to edge. From there, the ski takes over. You apply pressure while on edge and the ski carves a perfect arc. The skill of carving turns rather than skidding is one of the differences between intermediate and upper-level skiers. Once you feel a truly carved turn, you will have advanced your skiing a notch. (Provided you know what you did and can do it again!)

You can tell if you're riding flat by studying the tracks of your skis. If the tracks are deeper on the insides, your knees, legs and feet are rolling toward the center. If your skis are tracking heavily on the outsides, you're probably skiing bow-legged, an affliction more common among men.

A friend with a good eye, or an instructor with a trained eye, can pick up your misalignments by watching your knees as you glide on a cat track or a flat slope. The obvious signs: knees rolled together and large A-frame below the knee. More subtle indications on a steeper slope are skidded rather than carved turns, A-frame stem turns, skis sliding out from under you and edges that catch. Some women even bruise the insides of their knees.

Knock knees = injury-prone knees

Skiing knock-kneed is not a healthy way to ski. Beaver Creek instructor Carol Levine says if a woman is extremely Q'd, with her knees touching, rolling the skis on edge probably will place the knees in an unsafe, not to mention inefficient, position.

"Knees are supposed to bend *forward*, not side to side," Levine says. With some experts beginning to suspect that women's ligaments are looser than men's, skiing under misalignment is risky business, Levine warns.

In her literature review of female injuries, Suplizio found a study by Kentucky Sports Medicine, a private clinic in Lexington, that shows an increased incidence of knee disorders and injuries in women athletes due to women's misalignment caused by excessive Q angle.

Suplizio's preliminary research indicates a definite lean toward more knee ligament injuries in women than in men. This supports my survey of hundreds of women that shows knee injuries — sprains, twists, pulls and tears — rank as the most common skiing injuries among women.

The significance of this kind of information, once it becomes common knowledge, will be far reaching. Women skiers around the world at high risk of knee injury — from beginner recreational types to elite racers — will benefit. As awareness of women's biomechanics, and its effect on skiing, grows, the industry will be forced to change the way equipment is manufactured and to alter the way women are taught to ski.

And what about young girls just learning to ski? Does the Q angle affect their technique? Denver pediatrician S. Andrew Tucker says all females are born with a Q angle; as a young girl enters puberty, the angle increases as her hips widen. Physical therapist Conway says it's at about this age when young girls begin to experience knee injuries, usually from sports. Before puberty, however, the Q angle isn't much of a factor.

"I've never seen girls younger than 12 with knee problems because of a large Q angle," Conway says.

Center of mass

The second female biomechanical factor that gets in the way of women's skiing is our low center of gravity.

A man carries his mass in his upper body; most women, however, carry the bulk of their body weight in their hips and thighs. If your figure is pear shaped, you know this all too well. To make matters worse for women, the weight of ski equipment further lowers the center of mass.

While men reposition their center of mass with their arms, women control their center of mass through lower-body movements. As a result, women tend to sit back on the tails of their skis, where most of their weight is concentrated. This makes the tips of the skis float, or worse, cross or shoot out from under them. And because women don't have the leverage a man has with his upper-body weight, they try to balance forward by bending at the waist and sticking their butts out. Women who always are being told to "get forward," or whose ski tips wander or cross frequently, ski "in the back seat."

In addition, the majority of women are skiing in boots designed for men and they don't possess the leg strength to bend the hard plastic cuffs. It's like trying to ski with a cast on your foot. We need lateral support, but we also need flexibility in the boots to bend our ankles and knees enough to get us forward, centered and balanced on the skis. Boots that are too stiff keep the legs straight, pulling the center of mass off the center of the skis. In this teetering stance, the slightest ripple in the terrain will throw you backward.

If a boot is too loose fitting (another problem with wearing boots designed for men's bodies), the foot moves around inside, sacrificing the important foot-to-boot oneness you need for control. It's like trying to steer a car with a wayward wheel or ride a bike with loose handlebars. You can do it, but you lose precision and accuracy of movement.

Hip mobility

Women can do a helluva hula, but bumps and grinds can get us into trouble on the ski slopes. Because we *can*, many women rotate their hips to turn, instead of using their legs to create efficient edging. This results in overturning the skis and leaning into the hill as if rounding a corner on a bicycle, dipping the uphill shoulder away from the fall line. Women have a foolproof way of knowing when they're doing this: Our bra strap falls down on the side we tend to dip!

Bone length

Women are shorter than men. An average woman's tibia, or lower leg bone, measures 1.14

inches shorter than the average man's, according to Suplizio. Because most women are wearing ski boots that are really just smaller men's boots, the tops of the boots hit women higher on the legs, usually in the thick part of the calf. By grabbing us snugly at the widest part of our lower leg, the boot doesn't allow our foot to drop into the footbed, where it should rest for that important transfer of energy. Yet the boot we need to fit around the calf may be too big everywhere else.

Strength

Any woman who has been overpowered by a man knows all too well men are stronger. Men's strength makes them more able to use ski equipment to power through the snow. But women can make up for their lack of strength, which can affect their skiing. Bob Hintermeister, director of the rehabilitation and human performance laboratory at the Steadman-Hawkins Foundation, sums it up: "Given a man and woman of similar body size, the average woman will be weaker and more likely to suffer knee problems because of her wider pelvis and greater Q angle. Women can minimize these risks by optimizing their strength and getting equipment that fits and is properly aligned."

I will show you just how to do this in the following chapters.

Chapter Summary:
In this chapter you learned that factors other than athletic ability can hinder a woman's skiing: the Q angle, a lower center of mass, greater hip mobility, less leg strength and smaller size.

Chapter Three

Solutions

"First, I need new boots — mine are like bedroom slippers. Second, I need more lessons. Maybe I really need 20-year-old knees!"

— *Sue, age 52 from Colorado*

"I need a lot more time on the hill ... trying terrain I normally wouldn't try alone."

— *Catherine, age 24 from Wyoming*

"I need to find the 'key' to help me loosen up at the knees so I can ski the bumps and look fluid and effortless."

— *Jane, age 41 from Colorado*

Now that you've learned how your body structure affects your skiing, take heart. Using awareness, the right equipment and proper exercise, you can correct the unsound stance it creates.

Body awareness

If you're a long-time skier like me, muscle memory rules your reactions. Changing it requires concentration. Crucial to this change is being aware of your body and how it moves.

Teaching the neuromuscular system to develop sensory awareness for learning a physical skill is the theory taught in a program based in Vail. Founded by former ski instructor Margaret McIntyre, a physical therapist, Integrated Skiing is the only ski seminar in the country that teaches the Feldenkrais Method. It's named for an Israeli scientist and athlete who developed a process to improve body awareness and self-image through movement. His philosophy: *Nothing is permanent about our behavior patterns except our belief that they are so.*

Guided by this, McIntyre's six-day sessions combine indoor exercise and awareness training with on-slope instruction aimed at changing habits that hinder smooth, effortless skiing — a kinesthetic approach. "The ability to sense is directly related to the ability to move," she says. "If you can't feel something, you can't move it."

To create this awareness, you need to learn to feel. You've already taken the first step in becoming aware with the exercise measuring your Q angle. When you moved your knees to line up with your big toes and held them there, you used muscle and concentration to achieve alignment. This is what you must do when you're skiing. With repetition, it will come automatically.

One practice I found helpful on the slopes to prevent my inside knee from even thinking about turning in is to imagine the little toe of my inside, uphill foot touching the snow. Every time I do this, my edging is stronger, my knees more directed.

I've also learned to notice when I'm cruising that a breeze between my knees means I'm skiing dynamically and athletically, not knock-kneed.

Fore and aft alignment also ranks high on the list of important balancing techniques. In your skiing stance, focus on feeling the ball of your foot, then push on your arch, then press on your heel. Instructors will have you do this while skiing to make you think about the pressure points in a turn: the forefoot in the initiation, the arch in the belly of the turn, and the heel at the completion.

One woman who took part in my survey wrote, "I wish for feet perfectly parallel and close together at all times!" That's fine, as long as she doesn't try to accomplish this by *locking* her knees. Skiing parallel and skiing knock-kneed are not the same sport!

If you learned to ski in the 1960s like me, you probably use the Stein Eriksen style: feet and knees acting as one limb, like a mermaid. It looks graceful, and for women it's more comfortable because our knees want to stick together. But it's not as stable as the wider stance taught today. Called "the athletic stance," it gives skiers more agility and quickness.

I used to be proud of how together I held my legs while skiing. But instructors have convinced me that independent knee action and a wider stance make for stronger, safer skiing.

In the mid-1980s, I skied with a coach of the U.S. men's ski team who kept telling me to open my legs. I didn't have a clue how to ski like that, and he didn't have a clue why I couldn't!

Throw away your skirts

Denver physical therapist Bob Mathewson has a theory about why women keep their knees tight while skiing: Skirts!

Most of us probably learned the more lady-like position for sitting while wearing a skirt — crossing the legs at the ankles, knees primly locked. Girls learned that knees belonged together at all times.

Notice the sitting positions of musicians in a symphony orchestra: The men sit relaxed, legs splayed; the women present a picture of propriety.

Think about the daily functions we perform with our knees together: getting in and out of cars, sitting, standing, kneeling, climbing stairs, driving a car, going to the bathroom. No wonder we want to ski this way, too!

Social pressures have taught women habits that are ruining our skiing!

Equipment

While women can't restructure their skeletal system, they can compensate by modifying their equipment.

This is a good time to introduce Jeannie Thoren, a tenacious crusader for female skiers. When most women skiers were struggling with whether to buy in-the-boot or over-the-boot stretch pants in the early 1970s, Thoren was figuring out how to improve skiing by changing her equipment.

"Skiing isn't supposed to be a constant struggle or fight," Thoren says. She became convinced she could help other women with bodies like hers — queens of the Q angle — learn to ski better. "It takes one to know one," she jokes.

In 1990, Thoren parlayed her expertise into teaching one-day ski equipment clinics for women. With her husband as her technician, Thoren travels in her home state of Minnesota and in the Midwest, and plans to branch out to other parts of the country. Each year, Thoren reports, participation in her clinics doubles. Last season, 500 women learned to adapt their equipment using Thoren's ideas, which I share here.

"I get doctors, lawyers — women who are successful in every other aspect of their lives and in other sports," Thoren says. "It's a mystery to them why they can't do well in skiing. They tell me if I can't help them, they're out of the sport." Helping women learn to ski better has been easy for Thoren. It's getting the equipment designers, manufacturers and sellers to support her that's been hard. "Men, who control the industry, just don't understand it," says an exasperated Thoren.

This sounds a lot like male obstetricians telling women what it feels like to give birth, or how to breastfeed a baby. They can explain it scientifically, but they'll never know what it's like because they don't live in a woman's body!

Boots

Installing custom-made insoles with heel lifts, laterally aligning the boot cuffs and tilting the boots with a wedge underneath (canting) can change your Q-angle stance for better skiing — without a single lesson!

Custom insoles

Your first step in this alignment process should be a visit to a professional bootfitter, not a bootseller. He or she will make you a pair of custom insoles, also called footbeds, which are the foundations of building a better stance. These replace generic insoles that come with ski boots.

Lee Kinney, a veteran Denver-based bootfitter, believes custom insoles are key to good skiing. "They're the single most important thing you can do for yourself to get you performing correctly on skis," Kinney says. "Assuming you have a reasonably good boot fit, custom insoles help that boot transfer energy to the ski. The best ski in the world is not going to perform as it should if you're not transmitting to the ski the way you can."

Custom insoles correct a foot's pronation, a tendency to roll inward, as well as supination, rolling outward. This insole helps the foot maintain a neutral position in the boot, creating a solid base. Heel lifts help balance the foot fore and aft, which further aids the overall alignment in women. *All skiers — novice to expert, men and women — should ski with custom insoles.*

Shaft alignment

Aligning the shaft follows next. (This lateral adjustment of boot cuffs often is called "cuff canting" by manufacturers and retailers, causing confusion about what canting involves. The distinction: shaft alignment *centers the leg* in the boot shaft; canting *changes knee alignment.*) On more expensive boots with a cuff adjustment mechanism, this is done easily with a screwdriver. Many entry-level boots, however, aren't equipped with cuff-adjustment devices. They're made with the assumption that beginners, who only wedge or snowplow, don't need precise alignment.

But a beginning woman skier with a pronounced Q angle will find that poor alignment makes learning to ski harder. She, in particular, needs all the help she can get. Beginners with less misalignment probably won't need to think about cuff adjustments until they begin to parallel ski.

Canting

Under-the-boot canting involves placing a strip of tape or a pad of thin, plastic material as a wedge under the binding in order to tilt the boot. When boots are canted in this way, it realigns your knee position and changes your Q angle when you're standing on a flat ski. When canted correctly, Warren Witherell says, you don't have to *force* your knees further in or further out. You can stand naturally, and with the slightest movements of your knees, get the ski responses you're looking for: the "breeze between the knees" and just the right amount of edging of your downhill ski.

Do not try canting yourself. It requires a professional ski technician and you'll need to go to a specialty ski shop to do it.

Because binding manufacturers indemnify shops from liability, you may encounter some shop owners that refuse to alter bindings in any way. But technicians, who follow specific guidelines set by binding manufacturers and companies that make canting materials, can cant your skis without affecting binding-release mechanisms.

If technicians try to convince you that the combination of custom insoles and cuff adjustment is all you need, without evaluating your knee alignment and canting needs, go to another shop. They *know* the additional help of under-the-boot canting can be highly effective in reaching your goal of ideal alignment. They are either too lazy and don't want to deal with it, or they have been living in an ice cave on a polar cap.

Warren Witherell has been canting skis since 1968. He firmly believes, "The great majority of skiers require some canting under the boot soles to provide the most efficient alignment."

Canting is not new. I remember it from the 1970s. It faded in popularity for recreational skiers in the 1980s when the liability issue came about. Now, it's making a comeback, and women, in particular, should be delighted. Canting is the frosting on the alignment cake.

Warren Witherell and David Evrard say in *"The Athletic Skier"* that canting as a final step can make the biggest difference. "The first 80 percent of correction provides a 20 percent gain in performance," they write. "The last 20 percent of correction provides an 80 percent gain in performance." The authors arrive at this conclusion through extensive backgrounds in ski coaching, physiology and biomechanics. Both enjoy outstanding careers performing sports as well as studying them.

Since canting came out of the closet in 1993 with the publication of *"The Athletic Skier,"* more skiers are requesting canting. Evrard, a ski-boot technician, estimates eight to nine hundred shops across the country now provide canting services.

A simpler canting method uses interchangeable, wedged boot soles, a patented feature in the Daleboot brand (the only American-made alpine ski boot) and some Salomon models. After fitting the boots, the technician attaches the soles that give you the lateral correction you need to properly align each knee. The patent expires in 1995, so more boots with cantable soles will likely come on the market then.

Ideal alignment

Even the *slightest alteration* in finely tuned boots makes a difference in skiing performance. Think of how the steering in your car feels after the wheels are aligned: The car becomes more responsive, faster turning and better balanced.

Depending on the degree of your misalignment, you'll want to use one or all of these methods to reposition your knees to align them directly over the boots and eliminate the effects of an excessive Q angle. This change in stance will greatly boost your ability to flex your boots and turn your skis on edge, the first step in carving turns. This also helps with angulation and a more flexible torso. This principle goes for men as it does for women and will correct bowleggedness, too.

Cindy Suplizio, the biomechanical engineer, believes poorly fitted boots contribute to skiing injuries. "Women just don't make the adjustments to their boots and equipment that males either know how to do or don't need," she says.

A word of caution: Tony Osborn, a British orthopedic surgeon, says corrections should be made with care. "Most Q angles are from 15 to 20 degrees in angulation," Osborn says. "If you try to correct the full 15 to 20 degrees, then you are going to stress your knees, especially the patella-femur joint. I think you have to adjust, to a certain degree. You can do five to eight degrees quite easily; once you start going over that, you're liable to get into trouble."

Witherell and Evrard suggest that, in order to achieve ideal alignment, the center of the knee should line up 1/4- to 3/4-inch inside the center of the boot. In most people this requires only a slight adjustment, but it makes a big difference.

If you are really curious about your Q angle, physical therapists can gauge it by measuring your tibia-patella-femur relationship. A *goniometer* can take measurements from a long-leg X-ray or from bony landmarks on the body.

In Chapter Five, which deals with buying equipment, we'll talk more about canting. For complete information on canting, see Part II of *"The Athletic Skier."*

Getting the center of mass forward

Women can't redistribute their center of mass, but we can get it more *forward* on our skis. According to the Thoren theory, three tactics can be used to do this:

• Install heel lifts in your boots, as mentioned earlier, for better fore and aft balance. In addition, because women's heels are usually narrower than men's, they tend to float in the heel pockets. Heel lifts give your heels firm contact with the back of the boots so that you can lever the tails of the skis in the finish of the turn. They also raise the leg in the boot for a better fit around the calf muscle, which tapers lower on women's legs.

Thoren says heel lifts work every time for women who attend her clinics. "Actually," Thoren says, they work "125 percent, because some have been kind enough to get them for mothers and friends."

Heel lifts go hand-in-hand with custom insoles and are installed by bootfitters. Ideally, heel lifts should be *built into* custom insoles for a smoother and more form-fitting sole.

• The second way to get forward and in command of your skis is to press your shins against the cuffs of your boots. You learned this in ski school, but many women have trouble because their boots are too stiff and-or too loose. A lot of women ski in rear-entry boots that are more difficult to flex than mid- or front-entry.

Jack Mason, chairman of the Colorado-based National Ski Patrol, says women should keep their legs in the "position of strength" to prevent knee injuries. Also called the athletic stance, this is the centered, dynamic skiing position with knees flexed 15 to 30 degrees, positioning your *derrière* above the back of the binding.

If you can't get this much bend in your knees by pressing the boot cuff forward, you risk injuring your knees. You're also more likely to be thrown to the back of your skis and lose control.

One instructor taught me to stand a ski pole perpendicular to the ground, against the toe of my ski boot. If I could easily touch the pole with my knee, the instructor said, I was getting sufficient ankle and knee bend.

If you think your boots are too stiff or too loose, replace them with easier-flexing boots that have lower cuffs — boots made for women. Make sure you get a snug fit with the help of a bootfitter. (More on this in Chapter Five.) A temporary solution to a sloppily fitting boot is to add padding between the boot shell and liner.

• Lastly, bindings can be mounted 1 to 3 centimeters closer to the front of the ski than ski-manufacturers' guidelines recommend. (All skis show a mark on the waist, which corresponds to a center line on ski boots, indicating where the binding should be mounted.) Placing the boot's center line just ahead of that mark moves the mass forward *en masse*. It also places the boot where it really should be. Think about it: the smaller the boot — when matched to the ski's normal mark (designed for a man's longer boot) — the more likely it will be placed too far back!

Women who have attended Thoren's clinics say this adjustment cures wandering ski tips and creates more controlled turns.

Before you drill holes in your skis, this is something you might want to experiment with on snow, using demo skis with movable bindings.

Suplizio suggests that body characteristics like height, weight, bone structure and distribution of mass should be considered individually when relocating ski bindings.

Regard this tactic as part of a three-fold process of getting the mass forward. If you move your bindings, but continue to ski in ill-fitting boots that are too stiff and without heel lifts, you've only solved part of the problem.

As always, after you adjust the mechanical side, take lessons to learn the technical moves to go along with it.

Oh, those rotating hips!

A woman should re-center her center of mass in a turn by steering the skis from edge to edge with her legs, not with her hips. This difference is subtle. Skiers who do it right are those whose torsos face more down the fall line while their legs and skis move side to side, changing direction below the hips. Imagine the pelvis as a bowl of water: when skiing, take care not to tip the bowl and spill the water. It's really something you've got to feel to become aware. Take a lesson!

Again, sometimes the problem is equipment. Check that your boots are not too loose and that you are properly aligned. Levine suggests that using shorter skis or mounting bindings forward also can help.

Ah, that falling bra strap!

Keep your hands comfortably in front of your body about waist high and your shoulders facing a little more down the slope than your skis. This will keep your weight on the downhill ski, where you need it in order to carve turns. If you have your hands out in front and up where you can see them, your shoulders (and your bra straps) should stay up, too!

We are not little men

Does it make sense for women to have no choice but to use ski equipment designed for men's bodies? Until recently, manufacturers haven't produced equipment designed for women because it isn't profitable. Essentially, the needs of women skiers have been ignored. In Thoren's words: "The ski industry regards women as little men."

Slowly, the industry is responding. Manufacturers are beginning to understand the need for making boots that fit women's feet better and skis that are user-friendly for their bodies.

Although changing your equipment may not solve all your problems, giving yourself these mechanical advantages is a good beginning. It's like wearing black to look slimmer or getting a precision haircut that flatters ths shape of your face. Now, just do it with skiing!

Exercise

The last, and most important, solution to knock-knees due to the Q angle is maintaining strong leg muscles, especially those that stabilize the knees. (Exercises appear in Chapter Eight.)

You can adjust your equipment and align your knees. But if your legs are weak, you will tire easily, your knees will ache at the end of the day, and your knees will face increased risk of injury while skiing.

Chapter Summary:
You learned that awareness, proper equipment, adjustments to equipment, and exercise can help compensate for women's biomechanics in skiing.

Recommended reading:
"The Athletic Skier," by Evrard and Witherell. To order, write to The Athletic Skier, P.O. Box 21315, Salt Lake City, UT 84121. Enclose your name, address and $24.95 per book, plus $3 for shipping and handling. Or call (800) 223-4448.

For more information:
Margaret McIntyre's Integrated Skiing, P.O. Box 342, Vail, CO 81658; (303) 949-5529.
Jeannie Thoren Seminars, 2501 Jefferson St., Duluth, MN 55812; (218) 724-5809.

Chapter **Four**

Giving women the boot

"I didn't know there was a difference (between men's and women's equipment)."
　　　　　　　　　—Jill, age 39 from England

"I didn't select my own boots and skis. My male companion had them from a previous female friend—truly!"
　　　　　　　　　—Mary, age 52 from South Carolina

"I don't know about women's equipment. I would like to (find out). It might help!"
　　　　　　　　　—Lynne, age 38 from Massachusetts

Long-time Colorado ski retailer Steve Vorhaus believes "Everybody is searching for the Holy Grail in this business." How true! Nobody has been searching longer or harder than women. But we don't *know* we've been searching. That equipment could be a major barrier to our skiing hasn't occurred to us. Boots hurt? So what's new?

Sore feet are a regular part of life for women — like having cramps or bad-hair days. For generations, we've been squeezing our feet into disfiguring shoes and tolerating the pain. Why, we rationalize, should ski boots be different? And if we can't make a ski carve the way our instructor wants us to — well, it's because we aren't very good skiers, right?

The truth about alpine skis and boots is a good-news/bad-news story for women. The good news: Equipment makers are becoming sensitive to the anatomical requirements of women and designing products with us in mind. But don't think it's out of the goodness of their hearts. The industry figures it's time to cash in on our participation in the sport. Women now represent almost half the ski population, a viable consumer market.

The move toward ski equipment for women could have come sooner. Charlie Adams, director of research and design for Dynastar Skis, explains: "The materials and technology were there 10 years ago. It is more successful to do it now because we understand the need for products that will be better for women than their unisex counterparts," Adams says. "Everyone acknowledges the consumer thinks that way, so we are now marketing products that way."

The cavalier attitude of the male-driven equipment industry also has contributed to this decade of delay.

Denver bootfitter Lee Kinney says the outdoor industry has been male-motivated since the beginning. "A lot of salesmen really don't care what the needs of the customer are," Kinney says. "As women become more independent and not always seeking male counsel, you see more women on their own trying to find what works for them."

Peter Knights, Tecnica's vice president of product development and production, explains that times have changed. "Twenty years ago, women really didn't want to decide," Knights says. "They wanted to be *told*."

David Currier, vice president of sales and marketing for Volant Ski Corp., agrees women's needs have been ignored. "It wasn't until women made themselves vocal and showed they were willing to spend money on ski equipment that companies began to pay attention," Currier says. In 1993 Volant jumped on the bandwagon with the FX2L, a high performance, all-mountain ski marketed to women.

Now that women have proven themselves with their pocketbooks, choices are being offered in an unprecedented variety of skis and boots suited for women's skill levels and body types.

Here's the bad news: Actual differences in gender-specific skis really aren't that drastic, and most women's boots are only *half-way* built for us. Let me explain.

Skis for women

Labeling skis as "women's" or "men's" conveys the impression they're as different as bikini panties from boxer shorts. But they're not: A 140-pound, intermediate male skier can ski very well on a so-called woman's ski. (In the industry, the term politely used is "lady's ski.")

The ideal ski for the average woman is softer, lighter, easier flexing. By lightening up materials and reducing mass, ski makers build skis that enable lighter-weight, less aggressive skiers to bend the ski into reverse camber and hold the edges in a turn. Some add binding placement marks approximately one centimeter closer to the front of the skis to place a woman's center of mass more forward. They "feminize" the paint job and, *voila*! They're women's skis.

"Weight is what matters," explains Adams. "The biggest difference between a woman's and a unisex ski is in the flex distribution. Unlike boots, which have anatomical differences, skis for women are not different in shape or sidecut," he says. "Being softer and easier to flex could work for men and children, too. It's a marketing decision whether you say Woman's Model on a pair of skis. You can take any type of ski in our line. ... All you have to do to make them better for women is soften them up. Anybody who says otherwise is creating a marketing story that doesn't exist."

Mark Hunter of Kenny's Double Diamond Ski Shop in Vail recalls K-2's introduction a few years ago of the LTP, an easy-turning ski for women. It boasted a balanced flex (soft in tip and tail), foam core (lightweight), fiberglass torsion-box construction (strong), and was dolled up with "feminine" graphics. Yet it was identical to the company's hot mogul ski, the Gyrator. The difference? The Gyrator was dressed in black, came in more length sizes and cost $10 more! (The LTP is still around; the Gyrator has disappeared.)

It's important to know what makes up a ski and the type of skiing for which each model is designed. If you are a beginning-to-intermediate skier matching your *weight*, *ability* and *skiing personality* with a pair of skis, you're likely to end up with a ski designated as suitable for women.

If you're a strong skier and can work a stiffer ski, you might not want a women's model. For you, all the hoopla is a moot point. Your skiing ability probably is suited to a regular ski. You should be leery of a woman's ski that is too soft because it will steer like a wet noodle for you.

One exception: Olin's DTV, an all-mountain ski for women. Unlike other skis built to a man's prototype of 200 and 205 centimeters, the DTV was prototyped in 190 and 195 centimeters, the average length for women. Top female instructors — Carol Levine, Dee Bryne and Nancy Oakes from the PSIA Demo Team, and Ava Pfosi Merriam — tested the ski from beginning of construction to the end, determining optimal binding placement, sidecut, and flex pattern for all conditions and terrain.

"Right to the very end it has been their ski," says Olin rep Mark Lee. "This ski was built from the ground up for women. You can't beat it." The DTV targets strong, high-performance, recreational women skiers — a market neglected by ski makers.

Don't let labels sway your decision. The important thing is to mate your skiing with the ski that will help you produce your personal best on the snow. You'll learn how in Chapter Five.

If two skis don't work, try one

Women who have reached an impasse skiing on two skis might want to try a single ski. Think about it: You'll never have to deal with crossed tips, or skis drifting apart, or problems with your Q angle. Instantly, you'll gain the form you seek because legs and feet must work together on one ski, making you look as fluid and graceful as a mermaid, all the time; and two legs working together prove stronger than when separate and independent as on dual skis.

In 1992, I had a chance to demo the prototype of World Ski's new monoboard (not to be confused with snowboard). A mono*board*, with its wider shovel, is a much-improved variation of the mono*ski*, popular in Europe but never big in this country. This new version makes monoboarding as effortless as power steering your car.

Yes, I knew my feet would be locked in non-releasable bindings side-by-side on a single, wide ski. No, I had no idea how it would feel, or even if I could ski on it. The inventor, Ken Hunter, gave me a quick lesson, showing me how to use the outside edges because the ski has no inside edges.

It didn't take long to grasp the feel of the new — and rather strange — technique on the flats. I even got comfortable enough to take it into the bumps and powder. (With its wide shovel, it skims across powder and slush like a windsurfer!) The few spills I took consisted of nothing more than falls to the side of my butt — none of the yard-sale type I've experienced on two skis! By the end of the day, I had mastered a new, safe skill. And it was easy! Makers of the Uniski monoboard (similar to World Ski's, but with less sidecut and stiffness) say monoboarding's faster learning curve — for beginners as well as experts — eliminates many of the frustrations of skiing on two skis.

Ski boots

Boots and feet are a ticklish subject. Because feet are as different as fingerprints, ski boot manufacturers face a monumental challenge in designing for the masses. With proper boot fit *crucial* to ski performance, the task becomes even more significant. Building boots specifically for women can mean the difference in whether they advance as skiers or stay home. Boots too stiff, too loose or too tall for women — which means most men's boots — make skiing a lot harder for us.

Not too long ago, ski-shop salespeople told women to just add another pair of thick socks if their feet swam in ski boots. Now, they bring out boots with cushy liners that cradle the contours of our feet, and shells in eye-catching colors. We've come a long way, but we're not there yet.

Boot liners

What makes a boot a *woman's* boot? Most of all, it's the removable, pliable, soft liner, also called an innerboot. Bootmakers have put a lot of thought into making innerboots conform to women's feet, ankles and calves, which are different from a man's. (The term for a foot mold is "last." Remember it; it's a key word in this chapter.)

Here's a look at how women's liners differ from men's:

• They feature a lower cuff and a wider opening with less padding, to accommodate a woman's *lower calf muscle.* Because the average woman's leg is shorter than the average man's, the shaft of the boot needs to be shorter, too. Our calf muscle is not only lower, it tapers gradually to the ankle; a man's bulges like a nodule on a tree trunk. The flared cuff of women's models takes into consideration this shape, therefore helping to alleviate pinched calves. There are exceptions: A tall, long-legged woman might find a shorter-cuffed boot won't provide the support she needs. And calves can be as different as feet or faces.

• They are lasted (formed) for a woman's foot, which tends to be *narrower* in the *heel, ankle* and *Achilles tendon* than a man's foot of the same length. A woman's *forefoot* is *wider,* and her *toebox, lower.* Her *instep* is *higher,* and the area from *heel to instep* is *longer.* In a boot liner, these areas are shaped for a woman's foot by adding or reducing the padding.

• They feature built-in heel lifts or higher ramp angles for *forward* lean (remember where our center of mass lies?).

• They feature footbeds designed for women's feet. (The last two features become irrelevant if you opt for custom footbeds with heel lifts. Alpina's women's boot comes with a footbed that can be custom molded.)

There are variations from one manufacturer to the next in the lasts they use, just as women's feet vary. But at least manufacturers are starting us off on the right foot by creating an interior shape uniquely for women.

Boot shells

The shell of women's ski boots is another story.

Two components make up the shell — the upper shell or shaft, and the lower part, which encases the foot. With few exceptions, differences between women's and men's shells exist in the *upper shell only.* In women's models, it's made of softer plastic and, like the liner, closes lower on the leg, with a flared cuff.

A less-stiff upper shell makes it easier for a skier with less leg strength to push on the cuff, flexing it forward for better control, and offers more comfort and shock absorption. Beware of an upper shell that's soft on the sides, because it limits edging ability.

Unlike the liner, the second component of the shell, which holds the foot, *is made from a man's last.* Manufacturers conveniently call it a unisex shell — an oxymoron, because we know a woman's foot is different. Unisex implies it's suitable for both and that there's no need for a woman-only shell.

But there is such a need.

Shell sizing

When you buy boots, the bootfitter lifts the innerboot out (yes, it does come out), sets it aside and asks you to step into the hard, plastic shell. He (let's assume the bootfitter is a man) makes sure your toes touch the front of the inner shell while leaving room in the back. He adjusts the cuff until the space between the lower leg and shell is even all the way around. This is called "shell sizing." (Chapter Five covers bootfitting in detail.) The idea is to get the shape of the shell to match the shape of your foot. Always. No exceptions.

If the shell weren't crucial to boot fit, sizing it wouldn't be so important!

Think of the shell as the Jell-O mold or the bundt pan into which we pour our feet. It should fit like Cinderella's glass slipper, not her coachman's clodhoppers.

Lifting and drifting

Even when you get the liner to fit well — snug in the heel, ankle, arch, shin; wide enough in the forefoot — here's what happens: Depending on how hard and how long you ski, and how much you walk in your boots, the liner "packs out" and conforms to the shape of the shell. It's like sneakers acquiring the shape of your foot over time, defining bumps you couldn't see when the shoes were new.

This may never happen to a woman who skis moderately, six to eight times a season, and buys boots every three years or so. But for someone who skis a lot — 30 to 40 times a season — liners can pack out in one winter and get trashed in two.

When I bought my Salomon boots, I took them to my bootfitter for fitting, custom insoles and heel lifts. He put me in tune with the boots and I loved how responsively they skied. At the start of their second season, I began to feel my heels slipping. It was subtle at first but gradually became worse. So did my bump skiing. One day, as I buckled my right boot, I felt shooting pain across my instep. Had I grown a new bone overnight? I had to quit skiing after a few runs. What was happening?

I went back to the bootfitter. Indeed, the liner had compressed like a flat tire. My foot had shifted, and the hole cut in the plastic of the tongue was no longer resting above my high instep. The material in the heel pocket also had compacted, allowing my heel to slide around in the shell. My bootfitter was able to pad the sides of the heel and cut a larger hole in the tongue. This helped. However, I fear, the innerboot will soon break down to the point of no return.

"The inner will always seek the outer," explains Jeannie Thoren, crusader for women's equipment. "Until they design a woman's shell, it's not a *true* woman's boot." *When the shell is lasted for a man, even the best woman's liner eventually will become a man's.*

In search of the glass slipper

Engineer and consultant Jay White has been building a database of foot shapes dating to the 1970s in his work with shoe and boot manufacturers. The computers at his Foot Image Technology in Bend, Oregon, hold more than a half-million images of feet, plus the dimensions of every ski boot model on the market.

Each year, White and his researchers compare the new crop of boots with those three-dimensional foot images. *So far, says White, they have not found a single boot that addresses all components of the female foot.*

"It's our job to find that boot, and we can't point to one yet," White says. (As this book went to press, F.I.T. had not begun to compare data of the more than 400 models for 1994-95 season.)

Even with all the hype generated by the ski industry about boots for women and the slick ads of ski boot companies touting their "women's" models, White maintains, "Women's boots are adaptations of men's shells, at best. If a woman finds a boot that fits, it fits by mistake."

MEN
1. NARROWER FOREFOOT
2. WIDER HEEL

WOMEN
1. WIDER FOREFOOT
2. NARROWER HEEL

MEN
1. LESS ANKLE TO CALF TAPER
2. LARGER ANKLE DIAMETER
3. LOWER HEEL/INSTEP VOLUME PER LENGTH
4. LOWER INSTEP
5. HIGHER TOE BOX

WOMEN
1. MORE ANKLE TO CALF TAPER
2. SMALLER ANKLE DIAMETER
3. HIGHER HEEL/INSTEP VOLUME PER LENGTH
4. HIGHER INSTEP
5. LOWER TOE BOX

© FOOT IMAGE TECHNOLOGY

The reason: Ski boots (except for Daleboot) are made in Europe. Most manufacturers build shells to the likeness of a European *male's* foot — not the American foot, which, thanks to our casual, sporty lifestyle, is wider than the European's. To change boot size, they simply scale dimensions proportionately. But a downsized boot with smaller internal dimensions doesn't fit a woman's foot, which becomes wider and thicker as it gets smaller! In addition, scaling does nothing to account for a woman's narrower ankles and heels, higher instep and all the other peculiar properties of a woman's foot.

Jami Davis-Poisel, director of operations for Foot Image Technology, says women have never worn ski boots that closely resemble their feet. "Boot engineers think that women are more interested in colors than fit; and frills are more important than substance and performance," she says.

Instead of building a true woman's boot shell, bootmakers just add more bells and whistles, which they say will ensure a better fit. It seems as if they do everything *except* build a shell from a woman's last. "They're not addressing the issue," Davis-Poisel says. "They're dancing around it."

But talk to the boot companies and you hear a different story. "Almost every company has its own philosophy about what is going to fit a woman's foot," Davis-Poisel says.

She shells

Four companies maintain they've produce a woman-lasted shell in their women's models for the 1994-95 ski season:

• **Dolomite** says its "ladies" boots are sculpted around a ladies' last from the inner liner to the actual shell construction. Says the company's Jeff Mechura: "Dolomite ladies' boots are not just downsized men's boots. They are specifically designed and shaped to the anatomical differences of a lady's foot and calf."

Dolomite concentrates on the recreational skiers, who comprise 80 percent of the market. "As we progress, we'll move the ladies' line to more high-performance models," Mechura says. "We consider it an investment in the future."

• **Koflach** boasts "anatomical, power-control shells based on a woman's last" in its LC ladies' series. "It's a better fit," says Koflach's Rick Rush, "and it's more comfortable." He says the LC2 has ranked as Koflach's best-selling boot since the company started making shells from a woman's last.

• **Raichle**'s Flexon Lady debuted as the company's only boot with a liner and a shell lasted for women; Raichle produces no "unisex" counterpart for this model. While other models in the women's line include features designed for a smaller foot, they retain a lower shell lasted for a man.

But not for long. Explains Roger Beaudoin, manager of Raichle's product services: "The ladies' market is exploding, so we are moving in that direction [toward women's shells]. We are working on more ... so all of our women's models will have women's shells." Beaudoin agrees a complete boot translates into a complete fit.

• **Daleboot** also claims its 4.5-sized LT (low top) shell is based on a woman's last. This boot is equivalent to a woman's size 6-7. "We believe fitting a shell is more than just filling a tub," says Kurt Blaum of Sports Tech Ltd., distributor of the American-made boots.

F.I.T. picks

Keeping in mind that a good bootfitter (with a lot of time and ingenuity) can make just about any boot fit, Foot Image Technology recommends these boots with an average flex index (cuff bendability) of 16 (on a scale of 6-22) for the most common shapes of women's feet:

• **Dachstein Lady Pro:** This overlap for an aggressive woman skier holds a wide forefoot, and its larger shaft accommodates a larger ankle and calf. Best in short sizes.

• **Dolomite S92 L:** The classical narrow foot — narrow heel and forefoot, smaller lower leg — fits well in this all-mountain overlap boot. It also has a higher arch. (The arch is the part of the foot that is invisible in a wet footprint) This model was extremely popular in the 1993-1994 season, according to F.I.T. numbers.

• **Koflach LC series:** From the beginner-intermediate to a racing boot, five models fit the "tree-trunk" leg with a wide forefoot, large calf and high volume. (Volume is an area of space above the instep in a boot. A high-volume foot is thick from heel to instep and fills that space.)

• **Lange MID 6.1 L:** This mid-entry is for a fairly aggressive woman skier with a slightly narrow foot (B or C width) with high volume and a narrow heel. It's great for women's calves. The **Anthea 5.8 and 5.7** mid-entries for cruisers fit a wider foot (C-E width) with a narrow heel, high volume, and high curvature (needs extra little-toe room — a "Fred Flintstone" foot).

• **Nordica NX 8.5 L** overlap in the Syntech line for an upper-intermediate skier fits an average woman's foot with lower volume, narrow heel, average (not super-wide) calf.

• **Raichle Flexon Lady** overlap shell for intermediate to advanced skiers flares in the calf, features a narrow heel and ankle and lots of depth from heel to instep. It's tight on a high instep, though.

• **Rossignol Course Lady** is a high-performance overlap that might work if you're a strong skier with small legs, narrow feet (A-C width) and narrow heels. The **MID 8 Plus and 7 Plus** fit a slightly wider forefoot, average heel, higher curvature, fairly high volume.

• **Salomon** offers a broad range of boots for women. Worth trying in the **Optima series: EXP 9.1 Lady** and **EXP 8.1 Lady.** For aggressive skiers, these fit a B-D forefoot, narrow heel. Though not as generous in curvature, they get good marks for volume.

• **San Marco MX 8L** mid-entry cruiser fits a woman's C-D width, higher curvature, average volume.

• **Tecnica's TNS Lady** and **TC3 Lady** are the top-selling women's boots for aggressive skiers. Both overlaps, the **TNS** holds a narrow forefoot with high curvature and a narrow heel; the **TC3** holds a wider forefoot, narrow heel, and higher instep; the **TNS-AVS Lady** features the wide forefoot of the **TC3** and the narrow heel of the **TNS**.

So why won't *all* boot makers go all the way?

Manufacturers are shooting themselves in the foot. They acknowledge women's feet are different from men's and that fit is critical to ski performance. Yet, they are reluctant to design a boot that will provide optimum fit — thus, optimum performance — for women skiers. Their reason: money, plain and simple.

The ideal situation for boot manufacturers would be marketing a complete lineup of liners *and* shells sized and shaped for women, agrees Steve Kvinlaug, Alpina's product-development manager. "But as you might understand, that's a lot of molds, and ... it's a major investment," Kvinlaug says.

Mark Mahoney, product manager for Head Sports, maker of Head skis as well as Munari and San Marco boots, agrees manufacturers are reluctant: "Having a specific set of skis and boots that appeals to only 30 percent of the market is risky." (The women's market in the 1993-94 season was actually 42.8 percent.)

Says Tecnica's Knights: "It boils down to cost of manufacturing. In a high-end boot, you're talking $800,000 to $1 million worth of tooling cost....Out of 30,000 pairs of boots, should we make 10,000 of them ladies' and 20,000 men's? Or make 30,000, and whoever buys them gets the same boot and we don't get stuck with them in the warehouse?"

In 1986, Tecnica did break the mold by introducing the "first-ever ladies-lasted shell" in a rear-entry boot, says Joe Decker, a 17-year Colorado sales rep for the Italian company. "It was a huge hit — totally a fit situation," Decker says.

It lasted only six years. Why? Knights says the women's market didn't support it. Decker explains that the shell that replaced it, an overlap design, can decrease or increase volume, making it more suitable for both sexes. Because each shell comes with women-lasted liners, the company's position is that women can want no more.

"With the versatility of the overlap, you don't need to have a specific lady's shell," Decker says.

The dilemma over whether to design for women is clear. It's like deciding whether to get that two-seater sports car as a second car, or to buy a station wagon that will hold the whole family.

Read my lips: no women's shells

What will it take for manufacturers to make a complete ski boot? Says Knights: "Not unless racers demand an entire boot [woman's liner and shell] will recreational skiers ever see it."

But Knights isn't expecting that. He believes accomplished women skiers identify with hard-core skiing — skiing "like a man" — and wouldn't buy a woman's boot because they would perceive it as less performance-oriented or feminine.

"If I built a competition boot that was perfect for women in every way — with a lady's last and a lady's actual shell — the trendsetters, racers, PSIA women still will ski in a men's boot," Knights says.

Not so!

Every woman racer and instructor I talked to disagrees. Says Vail instructor Jean Richmond: "As a mechanical engineer, I would be one of the first to volunteer to test them," Richmond says. "The reason I don't wear women's boots is they're too rinky-dink. They feel like a kid's boot."

PSIA Demo Team member Dee Byrne, one of the world's most beautiful and skilled skiers, says the issue of boots "is a huge frustration for us. Most of the instructors I know are in men's boots because women's aren't strong enough." She doesn't think there are that many "macho chicks" that would refuse a good woman's boot because of its image.

Women racers are concerned only about what will make them go fast, period. German national team member Martina Ertl, who won the giant slalom in the 1993/1994 World Cup finals at Vail, says, "Sure, I would try them if they would be faster than the other boots. Boots are the most important thing. They have to be *exactly* like your feet."

Shana Sweitzer, a U.S. Ski Team racer, agrees. "If it [woman's boot] were made to race, I think everyone on the team would try it."

Nine-year U.S. Ski Team veteran Edith Thys says she'd wear a good race boot built for women. "If your feet are happy, you can put up with bad conditions and poor skis," she says.

So we end up with the chicken and egg theory: Elite women skiers wear men's boots because comparable boots for women don't exist. They don't exist because boot makers think elite women skiers won't wear them!

Some strong skiers even like a softer boot. Norwegian ski team member Jeanette Lunde says, "I used to ski on stiff boots. I got softer boots during the last few years because it's better for downhill. When you ski down you get more feeling.

"If Lange made them [women's racing boots]," she concludes, "I would try them."

NOTE: During an equipment clinic in the Women's Ski Experience at Sunday River, Maine, a Daleboot rep was amazed how poorly the women's boots fit. When he asked how many participants were happy with their boots, only one woman out of about 30 responded! Once they learned women's boots were available, all participants said they would buy them.

"Ad-ing" to the confusion

If you are confused about ski equipment, you're not alone. Women in my survey indicate they really don't know what equipment is out there for them. Answers range from "I don't know anything about women's equipment," (the most frequent answer) to an emphatic "No! I could not ski better in women's boots. They are just tuned-down men's boots that rarely accommodate the differences." Most are suspicious. Says one woman (who works in the skiing industry), "My gut feeling is it's [women's equipment] a marketing gimmick."

Information about equipment is not getting through to women. Manufacturers advertise in ski magazines, but my survey shows few women read them. It's not surprising. With articles like "Courting the Demons of Death," (*Ski*, March/April 1994) and "Bad-ass Bumps," (*Skiing*, December

1994), "Two Men, Eight Summits and a Game of Poker," (*Ski*, November 1993), and those relentless photos of men hurling themselves off cliffs, who can blame them?

If you can get past the Terminator trivia, however, ski magazines are great resources for teaching tips, resort reviews and other information about the sport — especially buyers' equipment guides published in season openers.

Recent ad campaigns targeting women by equipment manufacturers send mixed messages. A contemplative Kerrin Lee-Gartner, Canada's 1992 Olympic Gold Medalist, is featured in an ad for Salomon's high-performance Integral Equipe 9.0 racing boots. The double-page spread shows her in an after-workout pose with her weights, water bottle and ski boots.

The caption: "Racers have found a direct connection between power and speed." Over the bright, red boots is a single word: "These."

The ad speaks to women serious about skiing, *but it's promoting a man's boot!*

Consider the other extreme: The top half of a black-and-white ad for Koflach women's boots reveals a sexy black lace bra above the words: "Forget neon orange and bright purple. We've always thought black was a considerably more enticing color on women."

The ad continues: "Wouldn't you ... rather wear a high performance boot that was a bit more high fashion? Comfortable as flannel, sexy as silk ..."

The ad devotes four sentences to telling you about the boots, then asks, "Will they cause heavy breathing like the garment pictured above? Depends upon how hard you ski."

This implies women will feel as feminine wearing this ski boot as they would wearing the lacy bra. Now I ask you, what does any of this have to do with ski performance? Do we ski better when we feel sexy?

Lange produced perhaps the most straight-forward ad for women's equipment, so far. On the right page: the lower half of a woman's leg. On the left: the MID 5.1 Lady boot. The text pinpoints the boot's women-only features. It asks: "... How can they expect us to ski at the top of our abilities while cramming our foot into a man's boot?"

But the copy writers couldn't resist the lead: "Ladies, say good-bye to cramps."

Would they ever use men's jock itch as an advertising theme?

Shell shock

If ski and bootmakers want women to take them seriously and buy their products, they must take *us* seriously. Deb LaMarche, former U.S. Ski team coach, says racers don't put much stock in women's boots because manufacturers don't. "When manufacturers build boots for women that are the same quality as the men's, the women will go for whatever *fits and works*."

That's the bottom line.

As I see it, women skiers need to join forces. If we create a demand for equipment that fits and helps us ski better, manufacturers will realize the market potential. Jay White predicts immediate success for the first boot company that makes a boot designed for women's foot types.

How can we make a difference? By using our buying power. Start at your local ski shop. Tell the owner you'll buy new ski boots when he can sell you boots engineered from the outside to the inside for a woman's foot. Until then, *Nada*. Then, write or call the distributors. Tell them you're not interested in their product until they come up with a boot design that meets all the requirements of a woman's foot — in the liner *and* the shell. (Addresses, phone and FAX numbers are listed at the end of this chapter.) With the women's market on the verge of exploding, I believe you'll not have to wait long. If you need new boots now, try on the women's models recommended by Foot Image Technology. One may just work for you.

Born-again skiers

I am including this remarkable piece of equipment in this chapter because it's important for women with chronic knee pain, knee or leg injuries, or weak legs due to disease or illness. Women who have given up skiing or are thinking of giving it up for these reasons, should know about **CADS**.

CADS stands for *Constant-force Lift Articulated Dynamic Struts*. The name may be technical, but the results are straightforward: CADS dramatically reduces strain on knees, thighs, hips and lower back, consequently lowering the chance of knee injury in a fall. Even more exciting, CADS enhances ski performance and control because of the increased snow contact and edging power.

My friend Adele who suffers from chrondro-malicia, a knee condition related to the Q angle, was forced to bring an end to 40 years of skiing because of pain, even on bunny slopes. I convinced her to try CADS with me. We noticed the effect immediately. For me, it felt as though a giant pair of hands was lifting my butt, taking weight off my legs while at the same time pushing my skis onto the snow, making it easier to carve. I cruised faster and with more stability.

As for Adele, she kept waiting for the old pain to set in. It never did. We skied four hours straight, on bumps and groomed, and neither of us experienced tiredness in our legs. Adele was thrilled. I was amazed.

The system consists of a harness worn inside your ski pants, attached by strings and rods to pulleys screwed into the backs of your ski boots. (The strings come out of two small grommets poked into the seat of your pants.) It may look funny, but for those who otherwise couldn't ski, it's worth the hassle. Plus, it's a great conversation piece in the lift line!

Inventor Walter Dandy, who moved to Vail from Baltimore to market his product, has an inch-thick book of testimonials from born-again skiers. Their message: CADS allows infirm or older skiers to pile up vertical miles without pain or fatigue.

"The idea is brilliant," writes a 51-year-old woman who teaches physical education. "It counterbalances unnatural constant forward weighting of ski boots ... extending years of skiing by avoiding abusive muscle strain."

Says Dandy: "We think we have the highest customer satisfaction of any consumer product in the world."

Aspen, Vail and Ski Windham, NY ski schools all endorse CADS and offer instruction using the device. You can demo CADS in Vail, Park City, Deer Valley and Alta.

Chapter Summary:

With women making more decisions about ski equipment, manufacturers are beginning to pay attention to needs once largely ignored. In this chapter, you learned that few manufacturers actually have taken those needs to their drawing boards. Most prefer to test the waters with equipment "semi-designed" for women rather than sink money into high-performance products equal to what they call unisex products. Even though elite women skiers say they would use products designed for women's bodies, manufacturers are hesitant.

A single ski might be the answer for women who can't get it together on two skis. A device called CADS allows people with knee problems or leg fatigue to ski comfortably for a longer time.

Product information:

World Ski monoboard — World Ski, P.O. Box R3, Aspen, CO 81612. For more information or to order, call (800) 447-9754. A limited number can be found in ski shops throughout the United States. The board without bindings costs $499.

Uniski monoboard — Unique Ski Company, Inc., P.O. Box 639, Amesbury, MA 01913-0014. For information, call (603) 394-0058; FAX (603) 394-0115. The company is concentrating more on its snowboard production than monoboard production and may even change the name of the board. The ski with bindings costs about $575.

CADS — CADS USA, Inc., 2121 N. Frontage Road, Suite 160, Vail, C0 81657. For more information or to order, call Walter Dandy at (303) 476-4137; FAX (303) 845-8673. Also fitted and sold at Gorsuch, Ltd., in Vail. The CADS package costs $299; special ski poles that hold the rods cost $89. All parts are replaceable at no charge.

Ski-Ki — If you've had it breaking fingernails buckling boots, use this palm-sized tool for better leverage when tightening and opening buckles on all types of ski boots. Under $5. To order, call (916) 926-2600; FAX (800) 926-0004.

Ski boot distributors:

Alpina — Steve Kvinlaug
Alpina Sports Corp., P.O Box 23, Hanover, NH 03755; (603) 448-3101; FAX (603) 448-1586.

Dachstein — Jim Fitzpatrick
K/D Sports, Inc., P.O. Box 206, Banner Elk, NC 28604; (704) 898-4536; FAX (704) 898-6384.

Dalbello — Heinz Herzog
Dalbello Sports L.P., 72 Gray's Bridge Road, Ste. 1A, Brookfield, CT 06804; (203) 775-3353; FAX (203) 775-2886.

Dolomite — Paul Angelico
Dolomite America, Inc.
One Selleck St., Norwalk, CT 06855; (203) 852-1278; FAX (203) 855-1360.

Dynafit — Steve Patruno
Blizzard North America
Airport Industrial Park, 7 Commerce Ave., West Lebanon, NH 03784; (800) 654-6185; (603) 298-6000; FAX (603) 298-8643.

Heierling — Tom Slade
Heierling, 5415 Ridge Trail, Littleton, C0 80123; (303) 794-8935; FAX (303) 797-0546.

Koflach — David Donahue
Atomic Ski USA, Inc., 9 Columbine Drive, Amherst, NH 03110; (603) 880-6143; FAX (603) 880-6135.

Lange — Charlie Adams
Dynastar Skis, Inc., Hercules Drive, Box 25, Colchester, VT 05446; (802) 655-2400; FAX (802) 655-4329.

Nordica — Bruce Barrows
Nordica, P. O. Box 800, Williston, VT 05495; (800) 892-2668; (802) 879-4644; FAX (802) 879-1260.

Raichle — Roger Beaudoin
Raichle Molitor USA, Inc., Geneva Road, Brewster, New York 10509; (800) 431-2204; (914) 279-5121; FAX (914) 279-4877.
Rossignol — George Couperthwait
Rossignol Ski Co, Inc., P.O. Box 298, Williston, VT 05495; (802) 863-2511; FAX (802) 658-1843.
Salomon — Dave Bertoni
Salomon North America, Inc.
Eastern Customer Service: 400 E. Main St., Georgetown, MA 01833; (800) 225-6850; (508) 352-7600; FAX (508) 352-7478.
Western Customer Service: 1311 N. McCarran Blvd., Sparks, NV 89431; (800) 654-2668; (702) 358-1075; FAX (702) 358-8299.
San Marco, Munari, Tyrolia — Mark Mahoney
Head Ski Division, Head Sports, Inc., 4801 North 63rd St., Boulder, CO 80301; (303) 530-2000; FAX (303) 530-1418.
Strolz — George D. Donovan
George D. Donovan and Sons, Inc., 243 Lowell St, Andover, MA 01810; (508) 475-5062; FAX (508) 475-5868.
Tecnica — Peter Knights
Tecnica, USA, 19 Technology Drive, West Lebanon, NH 03784; (800) 258-3897; (603) 298-8032; FAX (603) 298-5790.
Tetra — Jaye Hayes
Tetra Sports Corp., 1006 West Walnut St., Canal Winchester, OH 43110-9757; (614) 833-6210; FAX (614) 833-5213.

Chapter Five

The buying game

"I don't know (about equipment). If I have a question, I ask my husband."
— *Melissa, age 23 from Texas*

"My feet hurt — they get cold, then numb. My boots are 10 years old, but I don't want to invest money in new boots because I'm not that good."
— *Jan, fiftyish from Colorado*

"I would like to know how to buy equipment that enhances my ability to ski."
—*Annette, age 29 from Tennessee*

Remember when one pair of sneakers covered a lot of ground? Not any more. We wouldn't think of wearing tennis shoes for aerobics, or running shoes for volleyball, or boating shoes for hiking.

The same goes for ski equipment.

Store racks are filled with skis specialized for bumps, cruising and racing. Certain boards perform better in powder, others better on hard packed; some are designed to take you anywhere on the mountain, on or off-piste. We can buy fat skis, short skis, long skis, hard skis, soft skis, torsionally stiff skis.

And boots! Have you ever seen such an assortment of high-tech hardware? After you check out what's there, it's a challenge to narrow the choice to the equipment that's right for you. But not to worry. After reading this chapter, you'll know exactly how.

Don't let someone decide for you! Only you can best assess your capabilities. You know in your heart how you look — and how you would *like* to look — coming down the mountain. One young woman told me, "I would like my body to face straight downhill, my legs [to] bend and give with the terrain with each turn. I ... want to look graceful, not like an abrupt, pole-planting skier who is trying really hard to get down the mountain. I want to look [as if] I weren't trying at all and it just came naturally."

Buy equipment with the idea you will improve each time you use it. Says *Snow Country* magazine's equipment editor, Jackson Hogen: "Buy for the skier you want to become, not the skier you are." This is excellent advice for women who tend to underrate themselves and take a reactive approach to skiing.

Don't be intimidated by men who make up 99 percent of the sales force in skiing hardgoods. Women are relegated to shades and suits instead of boots and boards. One lone woman, Karen Hedger, has been selling equipment for nearly four years in Colorado.

"Men don't trust me at first," Hedger says.

"After one man bought clothes from me, he stepped over to the ski rack and said, 'Now, who can help me with skis?'

"When I said, 'I'd be glad to,' he looked at me and said, 'You? You're kidding?'

"I asked him, 'Why are you surprised? Is it because I'm a blond or a woman?'

"He said, 'Both!'"

Do your homework:

• *Study* buyers' guides in the fall issues of the major consumer ski magazines — *SKI*, *Skiing*, *Powder*, *Snow Country*. Each uses a team of testers to try out the new crop of equipment and tell it like they ski it.

Recently, *SKI* magazine put more than 130 skis to the test. Women, usually racers and instructors, participate in these test and review processes and the magazines devote special sections to women's stock. (Critics of product testing, however, think Joe and Sally Skier should be involved, rather than industry experts who possess above-average skill and strength. If this were the rule, manufacturers could learn how the general public handles their equipment, especially at lower levels. Some critics also think the magazines enjoy a relationship with manufacturers far too cozy for objective testing.)

In addition, ski editors categorize every product, from poles to power bars, to make it easy. Some women's magazines, including *Women's Sports and Fitness* and the new *Skiing for Women*, publish reviews of women's equipment in the early season. Take advantage of these fountains of facts!

• Learn the terms. Know the difference between longitudinal and torsional flex. Find out how sidecut affects a ski's performance and why a ski turns. Learn about boot-cuff adjustments and forward-flex adjustments. Use the glossaries in this chapter to become an informed buyer.

• Spend a few hours in several *specialty* ski shops, where the staff sells ski-related products only, not guns and golf clubs. Different shops carry different brands, so don't limit yourself to one store. Talk with the most knowledgeable people you can find. Look for salespeople with experience, for those who routinely test equipment and attend product clinics, for those willing to give undivided attention.

Find your skiing personality

Make sure the salesperson understands your "skiing personality," Dynastar's Charlie Adams emphasizes. "The critical thing is to gain confidence that this [person] understands you as a skier."

Once skiing needs are clear, you can easily pin down the model. "It's more important to understand that a woman is [first]an expert all-mountain skier, and then that she's a woman," Adams says. "Once he understands that, he can go to the model. Then it's a matter of matching the right price tag, cosmetics and brand of technology."

If they know their trade, salespeople will begin the selling process by asking fairly standard questions to learn your skiing personality:
• Where do you usually ski?
• What kind of runs do you like?

- What would you *like* to ski?
- How many days a year do you ski, or anticipate skiing?
- What do you like/dislike about your present skis and boots?

If they recommend a ski or boot right off the bat before they know anything about your skiing, go to another store.

David Chutter sells ski and snowboard equipment at Princeton Ski Shop, a specialty chain well known to skiers who live in the greater New York City area. He says most male customers come in with rudimentary information gleaned from skiers' guides in magazines.

Women skiers, except for the more advanced, still rely on the sales staff, he says. "Beginner and intermediate women are totally in the hands of the salesman," Chutter says. "We do our best to inform them. But they must properly qualify themselves with us first."

How?

"Tell the truth!" Chutter says. "If a woman comes in and says she skis 15 days a year, but really skis five; or if she brags about going up to Killington and skiing Outer Limits [a black-diamond bump field] without stopping, but she's not telling the truth, I'm never going to be able to qualify her properly."

Skis

• *Short-radius turns*

For quick, squiggly turns or for skiing gates for fun, a **slalom ski** packs the liveliness you need. It can be demanding, but good skiers like it for bumps, trees and hard-packed; they hate it in powder and crud. Its carving ability comes from its stiff tail, fiberglass material and narrow waist.

- *Long-radius turns*

If you like to cruise on blues with long, sweeping turns, look for a *cruiser* or *giant-slalom* ski. Its softer tail and straighter shape make it stable at higher speeds and perfect for gliding, especially on open, groomed runs.

- *All-terrain*

Designed to go everywhere on the mountain, it's a cross between GS and SL. The versatile *all-mountain* ski brings you the best of both worlds, turning easily in varied snow conditions and terrain. *All-mountain extreme* skis are the four-wheel-drive vehicles you need for the gnarly stuff.

- *Bump bashing*

If you are serious about refining your bump skiing, buy a *mogul* ski. This ski hops from edge to edge; its softer flex moves you over and around bumps like a snake; it's lightweight when airborne. Stay in the bumps, though. True bump boards ski squirrely everywhere else. If you've perfected the technique, stick with a slalom ski.

- *Powder prowling*

Like your second car, *powder* skis should be your second pair. Wider and softer than any other ski, they're designed to float through deep snow and crud. The newer *fat boys* have twice the width of conventional powder skis and a bazillion times greater ease in turning. You'll feel like a duck when you get on packed, but if you're going to play in powder all day, you'll think you've died and gone to heaven! Buy fat skis 10 centimeters shorter than normal skis.

Ski categories

• *Racing*

If you're looking to buy racing skis, you don't need to read this section. You already know these skis are highly specialized for very strong skiers who want specific speed and turn shape. They come with GS and SL sidecuts and variations of both. Recreational Racing skis suit skiers who want top performance in free skiing and occasional NASTAR-type racing. Average price: high, $625; low, $330.

• *High performance*

This category fits advanced to expert skiers who might find a racing ski more than they can handle. High performance includes giant slalom, slalom, all-mountain, extreme and mogul skis and some women's or "light adult" models. Average price: high, $510; low, $275

• *Sport*

For overall enjoyment, intermediate to advancing skiers buy in this category. Many women's skis are found here because they are more forgiving than high-performance skis and flex with less pressure. Names such as "Elle," or model numbers with "L," denote women's skis in all categories. If you want a balanced-flex ski that's easy to turn for a lightweight, less aggressive skier, look for these terms. You can't miss them on the racks because of their feminine cosmetics — pastels and pretty graphics. Average price: high, $370; low, $190.

• *Recreational*

A novice-to-intermediate ski, this should be *rented* when you're learning because you may outgrow it faster than your pocketbook will allow. *Snow Country's* Hogen advises against buying beginner skis: "They will only help you remain a beginner." Invest in warm ski clothes and good boots instead. Average price: high, $335; low, $160.

Ski flex

The flex pattern determines a ski's ability to turn (longitudinal flex) and hold (torsional flex) under the pressure of your weight. (See the ski glossary at the end of this chapter.) Here's how you can check the flex of a ski before you buy it:

Longitudinal flex

- To test the shovel, stand the ski on its tail, against the side of your foot.
- With one hand, hold it by its waist and angle it an arm's length out in front of you.
- With the other hand, grasp the tip (facing you) and pull it firmly toward you while you push into the waist with the first hand.
- For the tail, hold the ski in the same position.
- Bend down to press the tail of the ski about six to eight inches from the end.

Test several skis to compare their flex. If the tip and tail bend about the same, the ski has a *balanced* flex pattern. If the tip bends more easily than the tail, the ski has a stiff tail. Most women's skis have a balanced flex pattern or softer-flexing tip, making them easier to turn.

Torsional flex

- Hold the ski's tail between your feet and steady the ski between your knees.
- Grab the right side just below the tip with your right hand.
- Place the left hand on the left side of the waist.
- Try to twist the ski by pushing with the right hand and pulling with the left.

If you cannot twist it, the skis will hold well in a turn. If you carve with your edges; make short, quick turns; or ski on hard-packed and ice a lot, you want torsional rigidity.

Ski length

Now that you've defined your *skiing personality* and *ability level*, you need to factor in your *weight* and *strength* to determine proper length. At one time, the rule was that the ski tip had to hit the wrist of the arm held straight above your head. Now, the model dictates the length: Skis for long-radius turns should be longer than skis for short turns or bumps. Don't be afraid of ski length. Remember, the task is to pressure skis in reverse camber so they grab and edge an arc in the snow. The longer the ski, the more edge on the snow for stability and control.

So, a 130-pound woman in good physical condition who likes to make sweeping turns on groomed runs should ski on 190- or 195-centimeter GS or all-terrain skis. If she's aggressive and likes to go really fast, she should buy the longer length; if she skis slow and conservatively on the flats, subtract five centimeters. If she skis bumps and powder every chance she gets, she should be on a softer ski in the shorter length.

Experts suggest subtracting five centimeters across the board for skiers older than 50. They think, once you hit that age, your muscles and mind turn to mush.

I disagree. Skiing is like riding a bicycle — you don't forget. A person who maintains physical strength through conditioning should base ski length on their ability and the terrain they ski, not their age.

It might be more appropriate for older skiers to buy longer skis because many give up knee-jarring activities like bump skiing, preferring fast cruising. You know best. Don't let a salesperson talk you into a shorter ski because you've lived half a century. Find a salesperson with gray hair!

Once you decide on two or three models that fit your level of aggression, ability and weight, take them for a demo run. There no better way to learn whether you're compatible with a ski. (Refer to Chapter Seven for tips on testing demo skis.)

Ski design trends

Ski trends of the 1990s are cap skis, fat skis and radically cut sidewalls, says Ski Industries America. The national nonprofit trade association represents ski, snowboard, and on-snow manufacturers, distributors, and suppliers.

Cap skis (see Tech Talk) debuted in 1990 and now, virtually every ski maker has caps in the market, thanks to customer demand. Cap skis claim to enhance a ski's feel by transferring energy faster from the skier to the ski's edge, improving performance.

Radical shapes on skis appear now in angled sidewalls, noticeably skinnier waists, flared and pointed tails, and raised ridges.

"Fat" skis continue to appear in manufacturers' new lines. This ski, popular for deep powder and crud, has beefed up business for snowcat and heli-ski operators. The ski's wide body speeds up the learning curve for powder skiing and brings more skiers to the steep and deep.

Some critics of fat skis maintain it's cheating to use them and argue that those who do can't apply the technique to regular skis. That is absolutely not so! The first time I used a pair of Atomic Powder Plus skis was in a powder clinic taught by the Egan and DesLauriers brothers (of Warren Miller fame) at Grand Targhee, Wyoming. I was transformed in one day from a petrified powder pansy to a hard-core, deep-snow, knees-to-the-trees powder junkie! Much of it resulted from the brothers' superb teaching, but I know I never would have learned as fast on regular boards.

I surprised myself a few weeks later at Winter Park when I sliced through knee-deep powder as light as whipped cream on my own K-2 KVC slalom skis, remembering all the motions that came so easy on the wide bodies. They're the training wheels for skiing powder!

Boots

When my mom took me to buy shoes when I was a little girl, the salesman put my feet in a big X-ray machine. Peering through the tiny window, I could see the bones of my feet filling the insides of the Buster Browns. The X-ray machine is long gone, but the desire for proper fit remains. Especially for ski boots.

For women, buying ski boots can be as scary as shopping for a bathing suit. (Or worse — if a bathing suit doesn't fit, you can always swim nude.) Your ski boots rank as the most important ski equipment you'll ever buy. Proper fit is crucial to alignment and performance. Most upper-level skiers know this. Research shows performance as the No. 1 criteria that advanced skiers of both sexes use when buying boots.

The second and third reasons listed by men in making boot choices: comfort and color.

Women, however, rank color ahead of comfort!

Fran Woods, technical rep for Salomon ski boots, describes the view from the bootmakers' end when it comes to choosing colors.

"Bootmakers go out of their way to see what colors are going to be predominant in clothes so they can coordinate with them," Woods says. Luscious jewel colors like pearl, amethyst and sapphire lure lower-level skiers, making color more important to them than function or performance.

Alpina's Steve Svinlaug believes women choose solely on color, not function or even price. "Women don't want ski boots to look like nurses' shoes anymore. They want beautiful colors," he says.

But skiing is not a fashion show, and boots should not be chosen as color-coordinated accessories. The best thing that could happen to women's skiing would be painting ski boots all the same color.

Jim Sczuka of Beaver Creek's Rightfit Sports says the way to choose boots is to look for fit, performance and comfort, and *in that order*. He calls boots the "transmitters."

"A boot should transfer whatever your leg does to the ski," Sczuka says. "If the boot's too soft, you can't feel it work for you; too stiff, you can't flex to control the ski; too loose, you can't steer."

In their desire to move their centers of mass forward, women should be careful not to overdo it, Sczuka says. "Too far forward locks you in a forward position, instead of solidly over the arch, and too much ramp angle puts you on the balls of your feet."

Ski boot categories:

• *Rear-entry* boots are found mostly in rental shops and in beginner models because they're comfortable. Also, skiers, especially women, find them easier to put on and take off. This once-popular style is considered less performance oriented and not as laterally stiff as the other designs today. These boots virtually have disappeared from intermediate and advanced models. Average price: high, $337; low, $192

• *Front-entry,* or overlap, boots with four-buckle closures provide a better fit for women, more support and performance, but can ruin a manicure! Average price: high, $498; low, $271.

• *Mid-entry,* or hybrids, combine the comfort and ease of rear-entry boots with some of the performance features of front-entry boots. Average price: high, $447; low, $280.

Higher-priced boots feature performance adjustments like cuff adjustments, forward flex, forward lean, micro-adjustable buckles and power straps.

Boot sizing

Sizing a ski boot is like taking a math test. Three standards are used:

- *Mondopoint*, the international metric system
- *U.S.* sizes
- Salomon's *Heel Instep Perimeter (HIP)*.

Nearly all women's sizes come in U.S. sizes 4-10, which fall in the Mondopoint range of 23-27 and HIP 290-340. Sound confusing? It gets worse.

Jeff Rich, *SKI* magazine's technical editor, a pedorthist (people who make and fit orthotics) and teacher of bootfitters, explains: "Despite the presumed standardization of ski boot sizing, finding the right fit is still somewhat of a crap shoot." Rich says same-sized boots from different manufacturers vary widely, as much as four to five millimeters, and something as simple as innerboot padding density can radically change the perception of fit.

"Ski-boot shells change only on the full size," Rich explains. "When you buy a half-size bigger, the shell's not longer. The extra volume of the inner boot's footbed tricks the foot into thinking the boot is longer!"

As sole length increases, so does overall inner volume. For each full size, length increases 3/16th to 3/8th-inch, ball and instep girth by 1/4 inch, and ankle width by 1/8th-1/4th inch.

So how do you find your size?

Rich advises working closely with a good bootfitter to find boots that wrap your foot snugly without pain — no matter the measurement.

Bootfitters

Finding a ski boot that offers performance and comfort is like finding a bathing suit that fits *and* looks great. But, like skis, the variety of brands, models and sizes makes it difficult.

Where do you begin?

First, ask around for a store that employs a good bootfitter. Ask ski instructors who they use at the resorts. In urban areas, you'll find bootfitters in specialty ski shops. Some bootfitters work independently in lab-type settings, fitting ski, skate and hiking boots as well as athletic shoes. Look for shops that advertise *guaranteed custom bootfitting, boot specialists,* or *board-certified pedorthists.*

Adopt a bootfitter as a friend. They'll listen to you whine about pain, cold feet and bad skiing. They want to hear about heels that slip, shin bruises and aching knees. They'll lend a sympathetic ear because your foot comfort and improved ski performance is their goal.

Some shops specialize only in ski boots, such as Rightfit Sports, a chain with stores at U.S. resorts in Colorado, Utah, Idaho, California and British Columbia in Canada. Buying ski boots at ski areas allows instant feedback. Fit-and-ski convenience lets you take care of buying and fitting during a single vacation, sometimes in a single day.

Do-it-yourself sizing

Some skiers heed the advice of computerized foot- and boot-scanning systems, such as COMPU-FIT™ by Foot Image Technology based in Bend, Oregon. The computer analyzes the dimensions of your feet, then compares them with all models of boots on the market and makes a non-biased recommendation of boots that best match your feet. *Snow Country* magazine has teamed up with COMPU-FIT to offer a dual bootfitting service by phone and mail: Call the hotline with bootfitting questions or to find out which of 80 ski shops around the country use COMPU-FIT. Or order their bootfitting kit, which includes a skiing profile questionnaire, diagrams to show personal problem areas, and materials with instructions for measuring your feet, ankles and calves.

Within 24 hours of receiving your information, COMPU-FIT will send you a printout of your foot data, a Flex Index (resistance to flexing), and suggest three to seven boots. The mail-order package costs about the same as COMPU-FIT's service in ski shops. The personalized foot facts can be helpful when buying other types of boots and shoes as well.

And, if you want to know which companies are producing the best boots for women, call the hotline and ask for Jami, Mugsy or Jay. Tell them you've read about COMPU-FIT in this book. They'll give you up-to-date findings on women's models, familiarize you with what to look for in women's boots, and help you narrow the selection by eliminating boots incompatible with your feet. You'll still need a bootfitter to tweak the boots you choose — few people, especially women, can fit into boots right out of the box.

Bootfitting

When you visit your bootfitter, he or she first will measure your bare feet and study them for anything unusual. By studying your feet and asking about your skiing personality, an experienced bootfitter will learn which boot will fit you best.

"A bootfitter should suggest a boot for you," says Chris Cumsille of Denver-based Christy Sports. "We know what fits a wide foot, a narrow heel, narrow foot, low- or high-volume instep and big calf. I can look at feet without measuring and tell what boot will fit. Every company builds a good product, it's just a matter of finding one that fits." Sometimes, this means shopping in more than one store.

When choosing a model, the bootfitter will "shell-size" your feet — the most effective way to match shell shape to foot shape. "The shell is the most important thing," Cumsille says. "It's the only way to size. You can't go by measurements."

To shell-size, place your feet inside the plastic shells, liners removed.

• For a **comfort fit**, the space between your heel and the back of the shell should measure about 1 1/2 inches. Bootfitters feel the area with their fingers and call this a two-finger fit. Your toes should touch the front. Most recreational skiers like a comfort fit.

• A **performance fit** measures about an inch or 1 1/2 fingers. Aggressive skiers choose this fit.

- A **race fit** ranks as the tightest of fits, requiring 1/2 inch or only one finger.

After adjusting the cuff alignment (if the boots have this device) so that the space between the lower leg and shell is even all the way around, the bootfitter inserts the liners back into the boots and asks you to stand in the boots. With the innerboot back in the shell, your foot should feel snug everywhere: Your toes should touch the front until you drive your knees forward. Then your toes should pull away, leaving a little wiggle room for a comfort fit. (A performance fit leaves less room; a race fit allows no toe movement.) You don't want any hot spots of intense pressure, nor do you want your foot to slip anywhere, especially in the heel pocket.

Bart Tuttle, Tecnica's bootfitter for World Cup racers, says women must be sure to size small enough so that the boot holds the foot securely with "no slop in there." A good bootfitter, he says, can configure a boot to reduce volume. "But," he adds, "most shops don't put in the time to fit correctly." This means if you don't speak up, you may end up with an ill-fitting boot.

Sue Booker, a 20-year veteran of ski and bootfitting at Loveland Ski Area in Colorado, holds the distinction of being one of only a few female bootfitters. Regarded in the skiing industry as tops in the field, she knows how the right fit feels.

"A proper boot fit feels like a firm handshake. It should feel like it's molded all around your foot and ankle," Booker explains. "And you need to be able to flex the cuff. A 120-pound woman can't flex a cuff made for a 220-pound man!"

Innerboots or liners use different densities of foam to achieve a balance of fit and comfort, explains pedorthist Rich. Expert boots (skill levels 9-10) use very stiff padding; performance boots (skill levels 6-8) use firm padding; recreational boots (skill levels 1-6) use more-compressible foam. Generally, the firmer the foam, the tighter the hold; narrow feet do best in boots with firm padding, Rich says.

As we learned in Chapter Four, you'll find most of the difference in women's and men's ski boots in the liner.

Bootfitting tips

• Don't forget to tell your bootfitter about chronic problems with your old boots, such as red spots on your feet or ankles, indentations, popping blood vessels or areas that cramp or go numb. Let him or her also know what you liked about the old pair.

• Wear or bring a pair of *thin* ski socks for trying on ski boots. (See Chapter Ten to learn why a thin pair is best.) If you borrow a pair from the store, make sure they're the same thickness and length as those you'll wear.

• Wear a skirt, shorts or pants that can be rolled up past the boot tops. Nothing should wrap your lower leg other than a sock.

• Try on boots at the end of the day. Rich estimates feet swell 5 to 7 percent standing or walking; 8 to 10 percent playing sports; 12 to 15 percent with excessive heat and friction. Altitude also makes them swell, so buy boots that will fit in skiing situations.

• Spend at least 15 minutes testing each pair to allow your feet to settle into the boot — walk, flex the cuffs, learn the buckle system.

• Remember, if you can barely flex a boot in the warm store, you'll never bend it on a cold mountain.

• Don't freak out if new boots feel a little too snug — a few days of skiing will break them in.

• If you own custom footbeds and heel lifts, install them in every pair of boots you try on. (When you buy new boots, your footbed should be reshaped to perfectly fit in the new shell beds.)

• If you haven't had footbeds with heel lifts customized for your feet, consider it a necessary part of the expense of new boots.

Custom insoles

We discussed the value of custom insoles, or footbeds, in Chapter Three and how they act as the foundation in the process of bootfitting and body alignment. Denver bootfitter Lee Kinney says it's like the old song about the knee bone connected to the leg bone, the leg bone connected to the ankle bone: "Any podiatrist will tell you what goes on in the foot affects the tibia," Kinney says. "When the arch collapses, the tibia rotates in ... the knee angles in, the femur rotates out, dropping the pelvis down." (The women's Q-angle, low center-of-mass syndrome).

"When we bring the foot where it should be, we align not only the foot in the boot, but the knee *over* the boot, and help the hip line up correctly," Kinney explains. Custom insoles place the feet in a neutral position, distributing pressure evenly over the foot and balancing the stance.

Heel lifts, companions to insoles, help balance the foot fore-and-aft and side-to-side, fill the void in the heel pocket, move the center of mass forward, and raise calves to a better-fitting, more comfortable position in the boot shaft. As we discussed in Chapter Three, women find heel lifts extremely helpful for bootfitting problems and ski performance.

Allow about an hour for fitting custom insoles and heel lifts. Materials and labor cost $50-$95, depending on brand and work involved. Difficult feet require more labor and material.

Usually custom insoles cannot be interchanged from old boots to new without reshaping them. When a bootfitter molds the insole to a foot, he or she also contours the bottom of the insole to interface with the top of the footbed on which it rests. If the old boot's footbed is shaped differently than the new one, some modifications need to be made.

When getting your custom insoles made, make sure the bootfitter takes this interfacing into consideration.

Canting

In Chapter Three, we touched on canting as a means of correcting the effects of the Q angle. You learned that wedges under the boots can redirect your knees over your feet for more effective steering, edging and carving.

I also mentioned that under-the-boot canting has gone under the table. Warren Witherell and

David Evrard, who reintroduced canting in *"The Athletic Skier,"* explain: "The obstacles to working with canting have been greater than the ski industry's commitment to it. Boot and binding manufacturers have been focused on other issues, and ... concerns over liability have scared some shops from mounting cants under the bindings."

With binding release and retention capabilities nearly perfected now, the ski equipment industry can be expected to pay attention to skier performance — and women's needs!

If you investigate, you're bound to find a technician — ski tuner or bootfitter — who will cant your skis. In Denver, Chris Cumsille says in one season out of 25 canting customers, only two were women. Not that women don't need it — on the contrary, it's the best way to align our Q-angled knees over our boots.

"Women either don't know about or don't think they need canting," Cumsille says. "Women come in and just want to get set up with equipment. "They don't want to hassle with it. Also, the money scares them away." Cumsille charges $50 per ski to cant. He says men customers, on the other hand, will to do everything possible to ski better. "Men show off more," Cumsille says. "Their buddies are beating them up on the mountain and they *know* what will help them."

In my survey, I found a link between a woman's level of ability and how much she knows about bootfitting and canting:

- Beginners are clueless.
- A little more than half of intermediate skiers said they had heard about custom insoles, only 17

percent said they used them. Fewer than a quarter knew about canting; only 6 percent said they used it. (When asked if they meant cuff adjustments or under-the-boot canting, most said they used cuff adjustments only.)

• Advanced women skiers were a little more savvy about getting the most out of equipment. Though more than half knew about the techniques, fewer than a quarter said they used either.

• Women who ranked themselves as expert skiers knew the secrets to ski performance: All but one were aware of these methods; all but three said they took advantage of them.

Determining canting needs

How do you know if canting will improve *your* skiing? This test is fun and simple: Grab a plumb bob, a pen and a partner. (A plumb bob measures vertical lines. Wallpaper and hardware stores carry them, or you can make your own by attaching a 2-foot-long string to the middle of a pointed weight.)

Follow these steps:

• Buckle into your ski boots.

• Stand on a hard, level surface like a wood floor.

• Have your partner mark the center of *knee mass* on the skin of each knee. Be sure your partner finds the middle of the *entire* knee area, not just the kneecap. (Don't be surprised if the mark doesn't land on the center of your kneecap.)

• Assume the normal skiing stance with feet parallel, about hip-width apart. (The same stance used in Chapter Two for measuring your Q angle.)

• Bend your knees as far forward as the end of the front of the boot. Do *not* force them to line up over your toes — just bend, then let them fall.

• Dangle the plumb bob from the mark on your knee until the weight settles in front of the boot sole.

• Mark the boot where the plumb bob points. Then, on the boot's toe, note a ridge or indentation in the plastic indicating the center.

• Measure the distance between the plumb-bob mark and the center line with a ruler.

If your pen line falls two-and-a-half degrees or more (about 3/4 inch) *inside* that center mark, you need canting under the inside edge of the boot sole.

If it falls outside the center mark or less than 1 degree (about 1/4 inch) inside, the outside edge should be canted. (Your bootfitter can help you convert inches to degrees.)

If you're testing with old boots, be sure the soles aren't excessively worn or warped. Witherell and Evrard suggest checking this way: Set the boot on a flat surface, like a countertop, and tip it slightly on edge. Let it rock back to center. If the sole is smooth and even, the boot will quickly settle. If warped, it will continue to rock. Your bootfitter can plane the bottom so that it lies flat.

Also, if you're using old boots, leave in custom footbeds and other bootfitting aids before you measure. Remove any devices added for canting purposes, but adjust the cuff alignment if this feature comes with the boot. Do the same with new boots.

Canting also can be determined in the shop by any number of bootfitters' measuring devices and a trained eye. **The Cant Company** and **Balance Tech** have evaluators that make comprehensive canting assessments quick and accurate. Like the Princess and the Pea, the tiniest change under your feet can be felt in your entire alignment!

Shops charge $15-$25 for this, but usually roll the costs into the canting fee. Canting product suppliers can refer you to a shop near you that carries their products. (See the product information list at the end of this chapter.)

Once your bootfitter calculates the degree of canting for each foot, a thin plastic wedge is fitted under the binding plate. Special screws secure the material and the bindings to the skis. Done properly, the placement of cants does not interfere with binding-release mechanisms.

A wedge under the binding is the most common method of canting. Interchangeable, cantable boot soles will become more accessible when the patent held by Daleboot and Salomon expires in 1995, and David Evrard says there's talk of cantable ski bindings. Also, canting by sanding or planing boot soles enables racers and those who use a variety of skis to switch without having to cant each pair. This method is the least desirable for recreational skiers because of its finality. Unlike a bad haircut, shaved plastic won't grow back if too much is taken off!

To cant or not to cant

Is canting really necessary?

Let me answer that question with another: Why ski with a handicap? In Chapter Two you learned that perfect alignment is the overall principle in ski instruction. From beginners to World Cup racers, alignment makes skiing *easier* and *smoother.* Women, especially, should use every mechanical advantage in order to maximize ability. Bootfitting services, custom footbeds and canting, will give you the edge you need to become a more powerful, dynamic skier.

If you wanted to become a gourmet cook, you wouldn't settle for flimsy pans or dull knives, would you? If you want to be a gourmet *skier,* look beyond the basics. These small additions to your ski-equipment cupboard will propel you to a higher level of harmony in skiing.

The Witherell-Evrard recipe:
- Awareness and assessment
- Custom insoles
- Fore/aft balance
- Cuff alignment
- Canting

Your bootfitter can do it all — usually for less than $200.

Participants of the 1994 Technique Weeks for Women at Beaver Creek learned the value of equipment enhancement. Following a bootfitting "chalk talk," those without custom footbeds (more than half) were fitted for them, nearly one third bought new boots, all had their boot cuffs adjusted, and all but one said they experienced a breakthrough in their skiing as a result!

Poles

Buying ski poles used to hold as much excitement as buying car tires. Until recently, a pole was just a pole. Now composition of materials (carbon, Kevlar, graphite and fiberglass) lighter and stronger than aluminum and skinny shafts add another dimension to the selection process. Composites come in slender, almost pencil-thin diameters as well as traditional (16-18 mm) size. Goode Technologies, which makes composites exclusively, maintain they are to aluminum what aluminum was to bamboo. The company claims its newest generation of material, Forlon, makes **Goode** poles lighter and three times stronger than aluminum, and more durable. Skiers say composites provide better shock absorption for their wrists and arms because of the shaft's ability to bend.

In the store, compare the lighter, slender models with standard size aluminum ones. Notice the swing weight and springiness on impact of the composites.

Expect to pay $20 to $140 for poles, aluminum to composite. The stronger and lighter the materials, the higher the price. Forlon poles cost from $39 to $69, a good buy for a Goode pole.

To determine pole size: Turn the pole upside down with the handle resting on the floor. Grab the shaft so the basket is resting on top of your hand. If your lower arm becomes parallel with the floor, the pole is the right length. Poles bought too long will cause you to sit back. If yours need to be shorter, don't buy a new pair. Poles can easily be cut down to size by your technician.

Grips 'n' tips: Poles with straps proved to be better than the strapless grip popular a few years ago. Many women are unsure about how to hold a pole while skiing. The correct way to hold a pole:

• Insert your hand *up* through the strap, letting it hang on your wrist.

• Wrap your palm around the handle and the top of the strap so the loop supports your wrist for a sturdy pole plant.

Some companies sell poles with special gloves that clip onto the grip, eliminating the strap. Others come with adjustable-height grips that screw up and down for skiing various terrain. Try out poles wearing your gloves or mittens to be sure the grip feels comfortable.

Tips can be the rounded button kind or a spiked ice tip. Ice tips obviously are made for ice and rock hard snow. But they can be weapons and tear clothing. Unless you ski often on those conditions, you probably don't need them.

Graphics: Painted surface finishes will scratch off; anodized graphics become part of the metal like a tattoo and will not fade or wear off.

Ski poles are the most abused piece of ski equipment. People toss them like rags into the trunks of their cars, weigh them down with luggage and bang them with a vengeance across their ski boot as though they were smashing a poisonous snake. Then they wonder why their poles are bent. A crooked pole will make a crooked pole plant.

To remove snow from your boot, a gentle tap on the side of the boot with the hard rubber handle of the pole will usually do it. For snow packed under your boot, **Skizone** makes a pole basket that doubles as a boot scraper.

Sno-Terminator ski boot scrapers attach to the top of your skis just behind the binding. They provide a little door mat to wipe your boots clean before entering the bindings. Ask for these products in ski shops.

Bindings

The original purpose of bindings was to secure the foot to the ski. Then foot release mechanisms were installed for safety, followed by step-in, step-out convenience and ski brakes. Now binding manufacturers are inventing ways to affect the way a ski performs. All six binding companies that distribute in the U.S. and Canada have developed specialized, mechanical, underfoot plates designed to enhance ski performance by affecting flex, increasing rebound, or dampening vibrations.

When purchasing bindings, ask about these features. If they don't interest you, don't pay extra money to get them.

Ess is the first fore and aft movable binding — ideal for women who want to experiment with moving their center of mass forward on the ski, as we talked about earlier. It can be adjusted in a few seconds, without tools, on the ski slope. Small adjustments allow you to find the Sweet Spot for binding location that provides the best ski performance in various snow conditions.

Racers know that riser plates (spacers about three-eighths of an inch thick) placed under the bindings lift them higher off the ski to create more leverage. Now women are finding them to be an uplifting experience. Ask your ski tech about adding them to your binding system, or check out bindings with this feature. **Geze** has the Power Leverage And Turn Enhancer (PLATE) that lifts the skier about two centimeters higher off the ski and has a built-in, one-degree-forward incline for a more aggressive stance. **Look** bindings raise the skier six millimeters with the C-Tech Power Rider absorber system.

Marker's Selective Control system allows the binding to be flicked into three different positions for skiing soft snow and powder, packed and groomed surfaces, and hard snow and ice. **Tyrolia's** Power Point device under its Free Flex bindings claims to increase the ski's flex, making it easier to turn. **Salomon** has three systems: Suspension and Driver for vibration control, and Quadrax for release in all types of falls.

Your weight, height, age and skiing personality determine bindings best for you based on the Deutsch Industrial Norm scale. DIN numbers correspond to the torque needed to jar the boot out of the toe piece of the binding. For example, racing bindings designed to release under racing stresses, may have a DIN range of 5-14. Beginner bindings and those for light-weight adults can have a DIN range from 2.5-9. A typical high performance binding ranges from 4-12. Standard is around 3-10. The higher the DIN, the more expensive the binding. Buy only what you need.

All binding companies make at least one model with a lower DIN-setting range for lighter weight adults and women. These cost from $150-$225.

NOTE: Shop for ski equipment early in the season when stores are well-stocked and sales staffs are enthused. If price is a consideration, shop the late-summer, early-fall or end-of-season sales. Choices will be limited, but you'll find outstanding buys on the previous season's stuff, from socks to skis. Be careful not to compromise what you really need for less appropriate equipment at a cheap price.

When to replace equipment
Skis
Like all good things, the life of your skis must end. But look at the bright side. You're not losing your favorite boards, you're gaining a pair of rock skis.

You'll know your skis are dead when:
- they lose their camber and spring.*
- they require more effort to turn.
- the bases show wear impossible to repair.
- the bases have been ground "to the bone."
- your technician tells you they're shot.

*If you can't tell loss of camber by skiing, stand the skis base to base as you would to carry them. Decambered skis fit together flat like books on a shelf with little room to insert a finger in the space between them at the center. New skis form a gap less than an inch wide. (It varies from model to model.) Notice the size of the space when you buy your next pair. Measure it if you have to, and watch it decrease! This is especially important if you buy used skis. Make sure the camber has not been used too.

Boots

After reading this far, you might be thinking about replacing your boots just to get a proper fit for better performance — a very good reason. Other reasons for buying new boots are when:

- you find yourself saying, "I love my boots — they feel like bedroom slippers."
- your bootfitter can't help you regain that nice, tight fit everywhere.
- the shell breaks or stress cracks appear, usually on the front of the ankle.
- the bottoms of the soles are worn out or warped (from walking on hard surfaces).
- your technician tells you they're shot.

Boot liners

If your shell is in good shape, but the liner has packed out, think about a replaceable liner. Most manufacturers keep some liners available for upper-end model boots. Check with any retailer that carries your brand of boot, or call the manufacturer's customer-service department. The liners wholesale for $75-$85; retail mark-up varies.

Better yet, *custom* replacement innerboots can be formed to *your* feet. They are the perfect solution for people with lumps and bumps and odd-shaped calves or feet. They're also warm.

Raichle makes the **Thermoflex** inner boot that can be custom molded and *re*molded from the top of the cuff to the toe using a heat process similar to one for custom insoles. This inner boot fits in any front- or mid-entry boot. It retails for $150.

Zip-Fit liners, as well as Rossignol's **Comform'able** custom liners, work in most overlap shells. Comform'able also makes a rear-entry model. While Comform'able is injected with polyurethane foam, Zip-Fit uses silicone, a gel-like substance that stays pliable and fills in all the little places and spaces of your feet. Both are expensive, around $200 plus fitting charges. But skiers who use them swear by their comfort, fit and durability.

Buying a new liner might be an interim solution while you're waiting for manufacturers to make that magic boot for women! Call distributors to find a store near you that carries them. (Information is listed at the end of this chapter. Raichle's and Rossignol's numbers are listed at the end of Chapter Four.)

Also, such things as buckle parts and power straps can be replaced on ski boots.

Bindings

Long before the first run of each season, make sure your bindings work. Bring your skis and boots to your ski shop for a preseason boot/binding inspection. The technician will test the release and retention mechanisms and check all components. If they fail the test, you'll need to buy.

TECH TALK
A SKI PRIMER

If you don't want to get buried in an avalanche of ski technology, these terms, courtesy of *Ski Tech* magazine, will help you become an informed skier.

ABS: A tough, resilient plastic used for the sidewalls, topskins and caps of some skis.

Cap: The latest ski construction genre in which the top and sides of the ski are covered by a seamless cap running from one edge to the other, tip to tail. Caps play different roles in different skis, from a simple way to finish and seal the ski to an essential structural element.

Camber: The "arch" under the middle of a ski between the tip and tail that distributes a skier's weight evenly over the ski. Reverse camber allows the ski to rebound after being pressured into contact with the snow.

Carbon fiber: Used for strength in skis as an additive in fiberglass cloth. Lighter and stiffer than fiberglass or metal but very expensive. Very strong in both tension and compression.

Core: Usually made of wood or foam, the core is the raw element around which the rest of the ski is built and in most skis the core's shape affects flex and weight. In skis that use a structural, load-bearing cap, the core plays a less significant role. While wood is the most common core, foam is increasingly being used either as the first basic building block or injected into the ski later in the construction process.

Dampening: The tendency of a ski to absorb vibration. Today most high end skis (as well as boots and bindings) include some element designed to reduce vibration that fatigues skiers and hinders performance on hard snow. Some companies include a rubbery layer running the length of a ski in or below the core. Others use rubber or metal pieces in different spots along the ski, like the tip and tail.

Extruded base: One of two different ways to produce polyethylene bases. More dense with smaller molecules, extruded bases are easier to repair but wear faster and hold less wax.

Foam: Usually polyurethane, the foam in cores of high end skis is durable, lighter than wood and doesn't compress.

In lower end skis foam is usually injected into a molded cap-type ski or mixed with other materials to form a light, inexpensive core.

Kevlar: An aramid fiber with very high strength and low weight. Excellent dampening qualities and toughness.

Laminate: A ski constructed of multiple layers of one or more materials glued to a core of wood or foam. Also called "sandwich construction."

Longitudinal flex: The lengthwise bend of a ski which creates the shape of the turn when pressure is applied. Usually a soft-flexing shovel will initiate quicker, slalom-type turns; a stiffer flex is better for longer-radius giant slalom-type turns.

Shovel: The curved up part of the front of a ski.

Sidecut: The hourglass shape of a ski from tip to tail. The more pronounced the sidecut, the greater the ski's short turn capability. A lesser sidecut will make a longer turning arc.

Sintered base: A high grade polyethylene base with longer, tougher molecules that hold more wax, usually found on high performance skis.

Titanal/Titanium alloy: Has the same stiffness as aluminum but is considerably more resistant to permanent bending.

Torsion Box: A ski construction method entailing wrapping a stiff material around the core. Some companies use wet resin-soaked fiberglass cloth as a wrap; others use cloth impregnated with partially cured resin. The method results in very strong, flexible and durable construction.

Torsional Flex: The sideways twist of a ski. A torsionally stiff ski has a greater tendency to hold and turn on hard snow as the tip and tail grab more than a torsionally soft ski which tends to be more forgiving.

Waist: The narrowest part of the ski just behind the mid-line and under the foot.

TECH TALK
A BOOT PRIMER

Don't buy ski boots without knowing their ins and outs. Read this glossary, courtesy of Jeff Rich and *SKI* magazine. Rich is a board-certified pedorthist, president of Custom Sports Lab in New York and chief faculty for the STN/SKI Master Boot Fit University for professional bootfitters.

Shell Designs —

External Tongue: A three-piece shell similar to an overlap boot but with easier entry and exit. Buckles close over a plastic tongue hinged at the toe to reduce interior boot volume.

Mid-Entry: A hybrid of front-entry and rear-entry, combining overlap closure with mechanical fit adjustment devices. Many employ a release lever or button on the rear spine, allowing the cuff to splay open for easy entry, exit and walking.

Monoshell: A two-piece overlap shell in which the walls of the lower shell rise almost as high as the upper cuff. The shell parts are virtually locked together, creating a stiff, responsive flex.

Overlap: Also called a *traditional* shell, this is usually a two-piece boot in which the cuff section wraps over itself and the top part of the lower shell; the lower shell closes down over the instep and forefoot, reducing volume within the boot between the shell, innerboot and foot.

Rear-Entry: These shells can fit a wide variety of feet because they generally have more interior space than traditional boots. To duplicate the retention achieved by buckles in front-entry designs, rear entries employ various fit adjustments. A series of cables attached to plates push or pull the innerboot down and back from the interior wall of the shell to hug the foot. Rear-entry boots are usually more comfortable and easier to put on and take off.

Innerboot Designs —

Innerboots or liners use a combination of materials and densities of foam padding to balance each skill level's need for response with comfort. Softer foam is used in sensitive areas near the forefoot, around ankle protrusions and the instep. More responsive, high-density foams, stiffeners or support pads are used in critical areas, such as behind the ankle, front of the shin, and under the heel where a snug fit is necessary. Novice and recreational boots often use softer foam to make the boot more comfortable and less responsive to foot movements.

Innerboot Features —

Flex Gussets: Channels or grooves embedded into innerboots around the ankles and over the instep to allow the innerboot to flex without creasing or bunching.

Injection Molding: Innerboots constructed by stretching a lining material and sometimes foam pieces over a last inside a mold. A soft polyurethane is then injected and left to cure. The construction yields a warm, virtually leak-proof innerboot.

Lasted: Innerboots made by stretching high-density foam padding and quality component parts by hand over a last (mold) and sewing them together. Seams are sealed with a waterproof material. The longer an innerboot is left on a last, the better it conforms to the its shape.

Preformed: These innerboots are usually found in less expensive boots. They use precut foam padding and less expensive component parts. They are sewn together by machine inside out and then flipped back to obtain the shape. Seams on preformed innerboots are sometimes left unsealed and are prone to leaks and cold.

Fit/Performance Adjustments and Features —

Achilles tendon volume reducer: A device that hugs the heel pocket to reduce heel lift during forward flexion.

Adjustable Arch: A foot support system that raises or lowers an arch pad built into the shellbed. Eliminates voids beneath the arch for better foot-to-ski response.

Cantable Soles: A removable sole that tilts the sole to align and support the foot and lower leg in the correct position for edging the ski.

Cuff Cant: Used to correct a bowlegged or knock-kneed condition. Mechanical device adjusts the boot's cuff angle, pushing or pulling the outside of the shell from the ankle area to follow the contour of the lower leg. A *dual cant* adjusts from both the inside and outside of the shell. Since the lower leg shape never changes, the cant need be set only once and should be done by a professional fitter.

Footbed: Not to be confused with shellbed, this is a soft, flexible prefabricated bed upon which the foot sits inside the innerboot. Also called *insole*.

Forefoot Volume Adjuster: Usually found in rear-entry boots, it secures the forefoot for more responsive control. Some devices merely lower a plate onto the forefoot to restrict movement. More sophisticated systems wrap the foot while drawing it to the inside of the shell to concentrate turning forces over the ski's edges.

Forward Flex Adjuster: A device that changes a boot's flex resistance. Numerous methods are used including springs in rear housings, block-in-channel devices located over the instep and cam-type regulators on top of front cuffs. When buying a boot, determine how important adjustable forward flex is to you and how often you think you'll want to change it. Also note that some systems offer infinitely adjustable flex while others, like the cant system, offer only a few choices.

Heel Height Adjuster: A mechanical device that raises or lowers the height of the shellbed to reduce volume between foot and shell. It can also increase the shellbed angle, increasing forward lean.

Instep Fit or Volume: Refers to the space between the shell and foot above the instep. Volume in rear-entry boots is usually controlled by tensioning a cable or strap attached to a flexible, molded plastic plate between the shell and innerboot from the top of the instep to just before the toe box. The plate is designed to evenly distribute the pressure created during closure and draw the foot down and back into the innerboot heel pocket.

Instep Flap: In overlap boots, a plastic flap riveted to the lower shell above a cutout on the instep of the shell. Provides increased lateral stiffness and power transmission while permitting easy entry and exit.

Shellbed: A sloping, rigid foam insert that rests between the innerboot and bottom of the shell and runs from heel to toe. Serves as insulation and provides forward lean.

Rear Spoiler: A wedge between the shell's rear cuff and innerboot. Used to create additional forward lean and reduce excess cuff volume for thin lower legs.

Power Strap: A strap that wraps around the top of the innerboot or shell cuff to keep it snug to the leg and increase boot-to-ski sensitivity.

HOW A SKI WORKS

I believe one factor inhibiting women's skiing is simply lack of knowledge of how skis work. Most of us aren't interested in physics, and few sales people take time to offer an explanation.

Consider the shape of the ski. It has an hourglass figure: narrow at the waist, widest in the shovel and wide again at the tail, sort of like a spoon. When a spoon sits on a table, only the bowl and the end of the handle touch the surface, while the middle arches above it. In a ski, this arc is called *camber*. If you press on the spoon just below the bowl, you can flatten the arc so the entire length of the spoon is touching the table. In a ski, this is called *decambering* or *reverse camber*. Now if you put the ski with its wide-narrow-wide sidecut on edge and bend it into reverse camber, the entire edge will follow a curved trajectory led by the tip of the ski. It has to. That's the path of least resistance. The harder you press, the more of an arc you make in the snow. This how you vary turn shape and get control.

Quite simple, really.

It's easy to understand why women, if they don't have the body weight and flexibility in their boot cuffs to pressure the ski into reverse camber, can't get results.

With improved materials and technology, skis practically ski themselves. Skiing can be more relaxed and natural. Pat Campbell, assistant director of the Jackson Hole Ski School, says today's style of skiing evolved in part because of the advance in technology of boots and skis. "The basic skills have been same throughout the years," she says. "Balance is the overriding skill. Then you've got steering, edging, and pressure. With changes in equipment, the emphasis of skills has changed. Now there's a *blend* of the steering, edging, and pressure." She explains in the past we needed more steering in turn initiation because we couldn't edge as early. "The skis were stiffer and didn't bend like they do now," she recalls. "The leather boots with a low cuff didn't offer as much support in the lower leg, so we had to use more pressure and edge at the bottom of a turn. Now boots are a lot stiffer, so we can edge and pressure earlier and with more support throughout the turn."

Chapter Summary:

With hundreds of skis, boots, poles and bindings on the market, choosing the right ski equipment without being prepared can be nearly impossible. To be an informed buyer, study the buyer's guides of ski magazines, learn the terms, talk to knowledgeable sales people in specialty ski shops. Then, determine your skiing personality and match it with the appropriate models. We covered buying skis, boots, poles and bindings.

The mystery in buying boots can be solved with the help of a good bootfitter. In this chapter, you learned how to find one and what to expect when selecting boots. You learned more about custom insoles, cuff alignment and canting, and how to assess canting needs.

Product information:

COMPU-FIT — Ski-boot fitting hotline: (800) 543-4311. For a *Snow Country*/FIT Ski-Boot Analysis Kit, send $24.95 or a Visa or MasterCard number and expiration date, with your name, address and phone number to: Foot Image Technology, P.O. Box 5475, Bend OR 97708-5475.

Balance Tech — distributed by Sports Tech Ltd., P.O. Box 233 Rochester, VT 05767; (800) 877-7776; FAX (802) 767-4606.

The Cant Company and **Zip-Fit** — distributed by Spirakut, P.O. Box 3430, Hailey, ID 83333; (800) 621-1657; FAX (208) 788-4783.

Skizone pole-basket boot scraper — 45 North Phyllis St., Suite 213, Mesa, AZ 85201; (602) 461-1936; FAX (602) 461-1907.

Sno-Terminator — distributed by Bolle America, Inc., 3890 Elm St., Denver, C0 80207; (303) 321-4300; FAX (303) 321-6952.

Chapter Six

Whistle a happy tune

"I've never felt I was a good enough skier to buy and take care of my own skis."

> — *Gloria, age 47 from Colorado*

"I don't think it's anything special to have your own stuff."

> — *Marina, age 43 from Holland*

"Equipment doesn't really matter. To me, equipment is equipment."

> — *Anonymous, age 21 from Texas*

In Chapter Five you learned the importance of finding a good specialty ski shop, one that deals primarily in ski stuff and has a full-time, knowledgeable, dedicated staff. You're in luck if a full-time, knowledgeable, dedicated ski technician works in the same shop.

A good ski tech is like your auto mechanic. You visit on a regular basis, pop in when you need a quick fix, get the inside story about new products and advice on upgrading. And, yes, occasionally you can blame your technician when you're not skiing well. Get close. After all, you're trusting this person with your life!

A good ski tech will keep your skis as smooth as a baby's bottom, the edges as sharp as a good kitchen knife, and the bindings as clean and as finely tuned as your car's engine.

"A well-tuned ski is a safe ski," says Rick Roberts, a veteran ski tuner.

Some people find their technicians close to home. Others take their equipment to a shop at the resort where they ski most of the time. How do you find the good ones? Ask around. You'll probably end up with more names of shops *not* to go to, but keep asking.

Ask men. The reality: men are more into the mechanics of skiing than women. Ask a good male skier who skis 30 times or more a year. Ask a man or woman who races — someone who loves competition and is serious about skiing. A racer's skill and a technician's knowledge are important elements of a winning team.

Ski tuning is a guy thing.

Right now there just aren't many woman ski technicians. (If there were, would backshops take down those revealing Lange Women posters?)

Nonetheless, Olga Jones, 29, who lives in Telluride, has been tuning skis since her high school racing days in New Hampshire, even though she found shops put her to the test to see if she knew what she claimed.

"They were very discriminating," Jones recalls. "But I've always been able to prove myself. I've had to work harder than the guys to get into the industry."

Jones is confident she's as good as the next man. "I know what I'm doing. I can do this job and be willing to learn what's new on the market and learn the mechanical end of it."

Advice to other women looking for backshop jobs: Be dedicated and determined. Find a shop that's open-minded, and that has invested in good equipment.

"They're out there. They're hard to find, but they're there," Jones says.

This is good advice for female consumers as well. A shop employing a woman ski tuner, a hard-goods saleswoman and "bootfitter*ess*" may be more supportive of women who want to take responsibility for their own skiing, rather than hand over equipment maintenance to husbands and boyfriends.

But if you find a male tuner tuned in to your needs, bake him cookies and follow him anywhere!

What to look for in the backshop

• *Experience and certification*

When shopping for your personal ski tech, find someone who demonstrates *experience* and provides *certification.*

Binding manufacturers require technicians to attend clinics and pass a certification exam in order to work on their products. Procedures must be followed and paperwork completed for each job so that manufacturers can protect the ski shops from liability claims.

Some shops, particularly those in large sporting goods chains, hire part-time schoolkids to work under a certified manager. I'm all for teenagers having jobs, but on busy days it's doubtful the manager can be looking over every shoulder.

And, when holes are drilled into the wrong place on your favorite skis, the mistake is permanent. Three holes and you're out: Safety standards allow only three pairs of holes in skis, whether it's intentional for three pairs of bindings, or whether it's carelessness.

If a tech does make a mistake drilling your skis, the shop might replace the skis, but you'll wonder about other blunders you can't see.

Holes for new bindings were once drilled in my skis so close to the old ones that on one ski they ran together when I was skiing. A screw popped out — and so did my foot. I wasn't hurt when I fell, but I was furious. When I went back to the shop, the tech just drilled another set of holes. I trashed the skis because I didn't know enough to demand a new pair.

• *Up-to-date machinery and tools*

You pay serious money for skis, boots, bindings and poles ($1,000 and up), so you want a serious ski tech to work on them. A tuner uses machines for stone-grinding, and files, stones and sandpaper for hand finishing.

Dull tools and poorly maintained machines can ruin your investment. Montana and Winterstieger make the top-of-the-line stone grinders, but the machinery is only as good as its operator. When you watch a ski pass through the grinder like dough through a pasta machine, you realize the importance of the hands that guide it.

• *Good working environment*

A sloppy work area with poor lighting and bad ventilation can also indicate a slipshod operation. Check it out when you're at the counter.

Sometimes it's not possible to see the backshop at all, so you must rely on what others tell you about the service.

What to expect from your tech

Times you should visit your technician:
- Installation of a boot/binding system
- Preseason binding and boot inspection
- Repairs and tunes
- Rentals and demos

When installing new bindings too new or old skis, checking bindings or releasing rental and demo equipment the shop should:

- *Check to make sure boots are compatible with the bindings.*

All boots and bindings are compatible; however, when fitting old boots to new or rental/demo bindings, the technician may find a warped or worn out sole, which inhibits binding function and prevents the brake from engaging.

Some boots have replaceable toe and heel pieces, but chances are you need new boots. On the flip side, new boots may not work with old bindings.

At the bottom of the toe piece of the binding is a Teflon or metal pad called the anti-friction device. Its surface should be clean and smooth. If it's torn or pitted, this could interfere with the release of the binding. These pads are easily replaced. Ask your ski tech.

- *Install the bindings on the skis and adjust the boots to the bindings.*

If you want your new bindings placed forward on the skis to compensate for your lower center of mass, or if you want a riser plate installed, this is the time to tell the technician. (See Chapter Three.)

• *Determine binding-release settings.*

This is important! Your *honest* input about height, weight, skiing ability and age helps your ski tech calculate the binding setting so that it can release in a fall and free your foot from the ski.

The comment I hear most from the rental and repair guys is that they suspect women "fudge" about their weight. This is no time to lie — nobody in the rental shop cares!

If you've gained or lost significantly over the summer, or if you're pregnant, your DIN setting needs changing. If it's a new binding, be truthful! An error in the setting will increase risk of injury.

You must also *accurately* assess your skiing ability. The International Standard Organization uses the following guide for skier types:

TYPE I SKIERS
- ski conservatively.
- prefer slower speeds.
- prefer easy, moderate slopes.
- favor lower than average release/retention settings.
- Type I settings apply to entry-level skiers uncertain of classification.

TYPE II SKIERS
- ski moderately.
- prefer a variety of speeds.
- ski on varied terrain, including most difficult trails.
- do not meet descriptions of either Type I or III.

TYPE III SKIERS
- ski aggressively.
- usually ski fast.
- prefer steeper, more challenging terrain.
- favor higher-than-average release/retention settings.

Once you decide which type fits your skiing style, the technician applies it along with your height, weight, age and boot-sole length, to the binding-adjustment chart to assign a recommended DIN setting.

If you prefer a DIN setting different to the one prescribed, you can change it yourself by turning the screws on the front of the toe piece and on the back of the heel piece.

Depending on shop policy, some technicians will adjust it for you, if you sign a release waiving liability. Others will provide a workbench and screwdriver but refuse to do it, rightly so. The last person to touch the setting is responsible if you crash and burn injuring yourself because the binding failed to release.

If a skier is 50 or older, the tech is required to move up the chart one skier code, lessening the tension of the binding. But this may be too loose for a very aggressive, all-terrain skier older than 50.

This happened to my husband, Howie, who nearly killed himself on a steep run at Snow King in Wyoming. Someone changed the DIN setting when his skis were tuned at a shop in Denver, apparently trying to match it to chart requirements. He is a big man, older than 50, and he keeps his DIN setting a notch or two high.

When he set a hard edge at the top of a steep section of trail, both bindings released, sending him on a slide that left him tangled in plastic fencing, which stopped him from slamming into a tree. His face was badly cut. Miscommunication was the culprit in this instance. Now, Howie never skis without first checking the DIN window!

- *Inspect each component of the ski/boot/binding system.*

There is a safety check list for boots, skis, binding toe piece, binding heel piece and ski brakes. A good technician should not sign off on equipment without components in optimum working order.

Tuning

Tuning prepares and repairs skis. As a rule, shops *do not* check binding and brake function with a tune, but you can ask if you're nervous about it. These terms will help you communicate with your ski technician:

- *Stone grinding* — a machine method of smoothing and buffing ski bottoms.
- *P-tex* — a polyethylene material that coats the base and fills gouges.
- *Bevel* — edges ground at an angle.
- *Edge geometry* — angles at which the bottom and side of the metal edge are ground to each other.
- *De-tune* — when the edge of the ski at its tip and tail is dulled rather than sharpened, to prevent skis from catching in the turn.*
- *Convex* — a base higher than the edges.
- *Concave* — a base lower than the edges.
- *Railed* — edges raised completely above the base.

The last three conditions are *not* what you want on your ski bottoms.

A *full tune*, which costs between $25 and $40, includes stone grinding, P-tex application, sharpening the metal edges, de-tuning tips and tails* and coating the bottoms with fresh wax.

A *quick tune,* or mini tune, costs $10 to $20, and usually means sharpening and waxing. My shop, Bevans Sports in Denver, will do everything in a quick tune that's included in a full tune except P-tex the base.

Sometimes, burrs or rough spots will form on the edges of skis. You can feel them if you run your finger along the metal. Instead of paying for a full sharpening, which you may not need, buy a small tuning stone at a specialty ski shop and remove the burrs yourself. I carry a stone in my ski bag with all my other junk and buff my ski edges just as I file my nails when they get scraggly.

Depending on snow conditions, skis should be fully tuned every 10-12 times you ski and quick tuned every five. Skis need more tunes and sharper edges for the hard packed, icy conditions. Softer snow in is easier on skis.

Check your tune when you pick up your skis. Scrape a fingernail across the metal edge next to the binding. If it doesn't skim off a little nail powder or polish, it's not going to hold well on hard-packed snow. Ask for more sharpening. Run a fingernail up the base. If you don't scrape off a little wax, ask for more. Don't be intimidated. You are paying for a service. Treat it like a dry cleaner.

Occasionally, you run into ski-shop guys with an attitude. Last year, while staying at a well-known resort, I sent my skis down for a mini-tune as part of guest services. The tune was lousy.

When I called to tell them the edges needed more sharpening, the young man shot back, "I think I am a better judge of that than you."

I'm sure if it had been a man's voice on my end he would've offered to re-sharpen the skis, no questions asked. The manager apologized, sent the skis back to the shop and offered me a complimentary tune the day I left.

To protect your freshly tuned ski bottoms, hook them back-to-back with Velcro holders that slip between the skis to keep them from scraping together and make them more sturdy to carry. Ask for them in ski shops.

*NOTE: Warren Witherell believes skiers who are properly canted and whose ski bases are flat should *not* de-tune the tips and tails. "De-tuned skis do not make good, carved turns," he says. Shops routinely de-tune skis and bevel edges because customers ask for it. Witherell says 90 percent of skiers are over-canted (on the inside edges) and have trouble with skis "grabbing" the snow. So they blame it on sharp edges. De-tuning serves as a band-aid to the problem. The real solution: fix the alignment and leave the skis sharp. "Virtually all skis are made to perform best with the edges sharp all the way to both ends," Witherell says.

Preventative maintenance

Doc Tully, a long-time ski technician, says if you're good to your skis, they'll be good to you. As with your car, a few common-sense practices on your part will help you keep your equipment and your turns in good shape.

Skis

Rust can accumulate on the edges of your skis and *dirt* will build up in the base.

Skis can rust when they are stored in a damp place like a basement. Dirt can be the plain-old household variety absorbed into an *uncovered* ski.

The best place for summer storage: in a ski bag kept in a room or garage with moderate temperature and minimum dust. (And don't hang skis by the tips: this can affect their camber.)

Before covering skis for storage, run a bar of paraffin down the edges or have your ski tech apply a coat of wax on the bottoms without scraping them. This will seal the bases from the elements during the off season.

Another problem is *de-lamination* of the ski base, which is caused by water seeping into gouges and unfilled holes. This can be serious, especially if the holes are near the metal edge, which can expand from freezing water and then separate from the base. You can prevent this if you glance at the bottoms of your skis after every ski day and, if you notice any deep scrapes, get them filled with P-tex right away.

Waxing your skis does more than make you go fast. A properly waxed ski won't stick to snow and will turn with improved control. The base will glide better and last longer. Oxidation from abrasion, air and sunlight can cause a white discoloration on the bottoms of skis. This means the bases are drying out and need wax. Water your plants ... wax your skis, advises tuner Rick Roberts.

You won't have skis to keep healthy if they get stolen. Always split your skis when storing them on racks or in the snow at lunch break. A single ski won't be as likely to be taken as a pair. A ski lock really keeps them safe. A cable combo locks costs about $15. To order, call (916) 926-2600 or FAX (800) 926-9904.

Bindings

The heel piece of the binding attracts dirt, especially if you carry your skis in a car ski rack. Keeping the bindings closed, or better yet, covering them with a waterproof nylon binding cover will prevent road grime and salt from getting inside the binding mechanisms. Always transport skis inside your car if there's room. Snap bindings shut when not in use.

For air travel, I stuff clothes in the ski bag to keep my skis from banging around inside and wrap towels around the bindings to protect the brakes during handling. The last thing you want on your first morning out is ski repairs.

At the end of the season, you should release the pressure of the binding by unscrewing the DIN setting. This will prevent the spring from becoming fatigued over months of non-use. Don't forget to reset it in the fall!

Boots

Plastic has memory. Keeping your boots buckled while not in use will help them retain their shape. As it is, women break enough nails spreading the hard plastic shell open. Don't make it worse by letting the plastic have a mind of its own.

Just as you avoid puddles when you're wearing your best evening shoes, avoid walking in your ski boots on hard surfaces like gravel or concrete. The wear and tear, plus dirt and gravel contamination of the soles, can cause the bindings to malfunction when they interface with the boots.

If you must walk on a surface other than packed snow, buy rubber walking soles. I use **Cat Tracks**, which clip onto the boots and protect the soles from deterioration and prevent slipping. (I've seen some nasty falls in icy parking lots.) Save the plastic wrapper so you can store them in your pocket or pack without getting road muck on your ski clothes.

Taking responsibility for your equipment puts *you* in charge of your skiing. The more knowledge you have about your skis, boots, bindings and poles translates into more control on the mountain. Try it ... you'll see!

America's best ski shops

(Compiled from 1,728 ballots — 1,276 from readers, 417 from sales reps, 35 from manufacturers — in a poll published in the January/February 1994 issue of *Snow Country*. Reprinted with permission from *Snow Country*.)

Far West
   Granite Chief, Olympic Valley, Calif.
   Sturtevant's Sports, Bellevue, Wash.
   Footloose Ski Shop, Mammoth Lakes, Calif.
   Mt. Bachelor Ski Shop, Bend, Ore.
   Sport Chalet, La Cañada, Calif.
   Newport Ski Company, Newport Beach, Calif.
   Village Ski Loft, Incline Village, Nev.

Mid-Atlantic
Ski Barn, Little Falls, N.J.
Langhorne Ski Shop, Langhorne, Penn.
Ski Center, Washington D.C.
Cury's Sport Shop, Ramsey, N.J.
Ski Chalet, Arlington, Va.
Willi's Ski Shop, Pittsburgh, Penn.
Nestor's Warming Hut, Whitehall, Penn.
Snow Country, Rochester, N.Y.
Windham Mt. Ski Shop, Windham, N.Y.

Midwest
Viking Ski Shop, Chicago, Ill.
Hoigaard's, St. Louis Park, Minn.
Bill & Paul's Sporthaus, Grand Rapids, Mich.
Ski Hut, Duluth, Minn.
Bavarian Village, North Olmsted, Ohio

New England
Strand's Ski Shop, Worcester, Mass.
Stan & Dan's Sports, North Conway, N.H.
Ken Jones Ski Mart, Manchester. N.H.
Aspen East, Killington, Vt.
Buchika's Ski & Sport, Salem, N.H.
Kenver Ltd., South Egremont, Mass.
Northern Ski Works, Killington, Vt.
The Downhill Edge, Burlington, Vt.
The Ski Market, Boston, Mass.
Action Sports Inc., Branford, Conn.
Competitive Edge Ski & Bike, Holyoke, Mass.
Startingate, Bondville, Vt.

Rocky Mountains
Colorado Ski & Golf, Aurora, Colo.
Greenwood's Ski Haus, Boise, Idaho
Gorsuch Ltd., Vail, Colo.
Boulder Ski Deals, Boulder, Colo.
Jan's, Park City, Utah
Alpine Sports, Santa Fe, N.M.
Kenny's Double Diamond Ski Shop, Vail, Colo.

Chapter Summary:

In this chapter you learned the value of a good ski technician, where to find one and what to expect. We covered how safety standards protect you; how to determine your DIN setting; terms and times for ski tuning and repair; maintenance and storage of equipment. And you learned if your ski shop is among the top 40 in America.

Recommended reading:
World Class Ski Tuning by Michael Howden (World Class Ski, $12.95)
Alpine Ski Maintenance and Repair by Seth Masia (Contemporary Books, $9.95)

Product Information:
Cat Tracks — distributed by Seirus; Rocky Mountains: 2200 West Alexander, SLC, UT 84119; (801) 972-8849; Pacific: 9076 Carroll Way, San Diego, CA 92121; (619) 271-7797.

The Third Hand catalog—the company carries mostly tuning tools, but also sells great little inventions for skiers, many of which I mention in this book. To order the catalog, which is chock full of useful information, call (916) 926-2600 or FAX (800) 926-9904. Jack Moore would love to send you one!

Chapter Seven

The rental maze

"My boots were not only uncomfortable but really a misfit the first time I rented."
— *Becky, age 42 from Colorado*

"I'm so confused about equipment. I've gone to what I thought were reliable ski shops and I get a different story every time."
— *Judy, age 42 from California*

"I have canting on my boots, but I have no idea how to use it."
— *Cyndi, age 31 from Colorado*

M ost women know as much about renting ski equipment as they know about repairing their cars. Don't let rental shops fool you. From shop to shop and resort to resort, you'll find great variances. Cost, quality and variety of rental packages are determined by the store's owner.

"There are no industry standards for renting," according to Mike Weber, of Mogul Mike's ski shops in Summit County, Colorado. "You just have to *trust* the shop."

"Trust me." Are these not the two most dreaded words a woman hears from a man? Yet women walk into rental shops and give themselves over to the mercy of the young men behind the counter.

Most rental staffs take the position, "What you don't know won't hurt you." Skiers, who don't bother to learn about equipment, can end up with ill-fitting boots and trashed-out skis. It's up to you to determine what you need and know what you're getting.

Jay Gump at Blue River Sports, a rental shop in Breckenridge, says fitting someone in rentals isn't difficult. Before recommending equipment, he says, the rental tech should ask the customer about experience and skiing preferences. the same procedure as when you buy new products.

"After I talk to someone for only a few minutes I can tell what kind of skier they are," Gump says. "Sometimes it's just their tone of voice, sometimes it's their attitude."

Telling truthfully how you like to ski and where, and revealing boot problems you have experienced will help the rental clerk make a more accurate decision about you. If he or she shows an unwillingness to chat with you about your skiing, go to another shop.

Let's discuss what you need to know.

Quality and variety

A rental package includes skis, boots and poles. If you're a never-ever, rent all three until you decide whether you're going to stick with skiing. Then buy intermediate-level equipment you can grow into as skills improve.

Traveling skiers often rent skis to avoid the hassle of baggage, and carry their own boots on the plane. Some people who ski only one week a year prefer to rent rather than invest in gear. Then there are skiers who want to sample new skis for fun or for serious comparative shopping.

Ski shops try to cover all the bases by carrying several classes of equipment. Categories can include *budget, standard, sport, high performance* and *demo,* or some variation of these.

What one shop calls standard, another might call budget, which can mean anything from two- to eight-year-old skis. Some shops use budget stock of old, untuned skis to sell upgrades to a standard category "for a few dollars more." Beware of how crummy the crummiest gear is! Don't request the standard or basic package. Find out what the range is and ask to see the equipment. Performance class is a good bet.

Dave's Ski Shops in Tahoe City and Truckee, California, carry a standard package of low-end equipment and a demo package. The demo class includes performance, high performance and exotic (no kidding!). Mogul Mike's keeps it simple: standard and high performance. Blue River Sports stocks recreation, deluxe, performance and competition.

(Refer to Chapter Five about matching your skiing personality with ski and boot categories.)

Boots

Skiing in rental boots is like walking in someone else's shoes — they may be your *size*, but they just don't fit right! Avoid it if you can.

If you must rent boots, everything you learned about buying boots and bootfitting should be applied. You'll find fewer choices of models in rental boots and, in some cases, less quality. Shop owners carry easy-to-fit boots they know will offer the most comfort, but not necessarily the best performance. Boots on the low end of the rental scale are usually rear-entry models lacking any adjustments. Avoid these.

Even if you're a beginner, try to find boots with alignment features. It may be hard, manufacturers think lower-level skiers don't need boot adjustments. But starting off with proper alignment, fit and comfort is as important for a skier as learning how to hold a racquet is for a tennis player.

Don't accept a boot that hurts, or a cuff you can't bend. If you have to clamp down on the buckles to the point of pain to make the boots snug, go to another shop. An ill-fitting boot can ruin your day!

Wear or bring your own ski socks. The socks used for fitting boots in the rental shop may not be the same thickness as yours.

Ask lots of questions about fitting and alignment. I observed one woman step into a basic boot and say, "It's too big in the heel." The rental tech diverted her attention to her toes and never did address the heel problem. Worse, the woman neglected to bring it up again! She paid him, and went to try skiing on those improper-fitting boots. She's probably taken up golf.

Some shops that specialize only in rentals, such as Blue River Sports, offer excellent boot-fitting. They use pronation pads, arch supports and heel lifts to get it right, and rent only new boots in all but their lowest packages.

If you find most rental boots too stiff, ask for women's boots. A specialty shop with a large inventory may carry them. Chances are they will flex easier and fit better too. Make sure the boots are new.

Some shops try to pass off older models as women's boots because the shell is a pastel color. Call them on it! Let them know *you* know the difference. Ask about woman-lasted liners, flexibility and cuff height. The reason most shops don't carry women's boots is because they claim there isn't enough demand. Let's create it!

Skis

After you go through the initial Q&A drill, the rental tech will ask what length of ski you want. Women seem to be intimidated with anything longer than 170 cm. But remember, length is determined by weight, ability and type of ski, not your height.

Be honest about your weight and ability when it comes to filling out the form for your DIN setting. Every rental binding must be reset for each renter's requirements. (See Chapter Six.)

You also should check the skis for a good tune. The bottoms of rental skis usually show plenty of wear and tear underneath the P-tex. But if they feel smooth and waxed, and the edges feel sharp, they'll do.

Managers and owners of most rental shops want their customers happy. A skier's comfort and enjoyment is at the mercy of their employees. Consumers must be reasonable, too.

Weber recalls a teenage girl at the start of a ski vacation asking for purple boots to match her skis. It happened that the purple boots were a terrible fit and, despite Weber's recommendations, she insisted the boots were for her.

"I know she must have been uncomfortable the whole vacation," Weber says. "We can recommend all day, but if the customer won't listen...."

Poles

Rental poles are usually of one variety and your choices are limited. Refer to Chapter Five for selecting the right length.

Cost

Ski-area rental shops are more expensive than shops in ski towns, or cities removed from skiing. You pay for the convenience of not having to lug skis, boots and poles farther than, say, 20 yards. And you pay for the accessibility during the day that allows you to switch boots that are uncomfortable or skis that need sharper edges. But keep in mind ski-area rental shops maintain an assembly-line approach to fitting customers, due to sheer numbers. You might not get the personal attention you want and need.

The best time to line up equipment is the evening before you ski, when you're more likely to find someone who can help you through the process. Late morning, 10:30 or 11 a.m., and mid-afternoon, before the end of the ski day, are good times, too. Avoid Saturday and Sunday mornings.

Prices for rentals vary greatly. Where the lift ticket costs a lot, you can bet the rentals are high too. The *lowest* price of base shops at Killington Resort in Central Vermont are higher than the highest price at Park City, Utah's Sea & Ski!

In similar ski-country towns, Mogul Mike's charges $6 to $10.95. Dave's Ski Shop offers packages from $14 to $29 (for that exotic ski). Multi-day and multi-person rates are lower than single-day/one-person rates, and prices take a hike in high season. Sales tax is charged on rentals in states where applicable.

Damage deposits are covered with a credit-card imprint that the shop destroys when you return equipment intact. If you don't have a card, a driver's license will normally do.

One call does it all

Arranging equipment needs by telephone is helpful, especially for families and large groups. Some resorts' central reservations will reserve rentals, and some shops provide 800 numbers. If you know exactly what you want, requesting in advance saves time and ensures you'll get what you need.

You can also call National Sports Rental, "Your Winter Sports Concierge," at 800-765-2SKI. As the "FTD florist" of ski rentals, NSR makes reservations for customers in 90 shops at resorts throughout the U. S. and Canada. After spending three years setting up the system, owner George Koutsakis possesses a local's knowledge of the best shops.

Depending on the resort and the shop, Koutsakis charges an average of $10, $15 and $20 a day for three classes of equipment. A bulk rate is available for more people and days.

As with lodging reservations, each customer receives a confirmation of the order and a map showing the location of the shop. Questions asked by NSR eliminate most chances of ill-fitting boots. If that does happen, the shop and NSR will find a replacement pair.

Demo

Most retail shops offer the option of testing skis before buying, and then apply the cost of demos to the cost of new skis. This is a great opportunity to match your skills with the right skis, but taking skis for a test drive can be tricky. Women tell me they have a hard time determining what makes a good run: Is it the skis, the snow, or the driver? Here are some rules to follow for the ideal way to demo:

• Watch for Demo Days at ski areas when the public can test skis from manufacturers' vans of inventory at the base. Same-day testing can also be done from ski-area rental or retail shops.

• Ski one long run on the same trail, the same day, on several pairs of skis. This way you can compare based on similar surface conditions.

• Pick a run with varied terrain to test how the skis perform on the flats vs. steeper pitches and mogul fields. Or take several trails with this kind of terrain.

• Test mogul skis on moguls, powder skis in powder, and cruisers on wide, open fields. Use the ski for the purpose for which it is designed. If it's an all-mountain ski, take it everywhere.

• Give your full attention to the task at hand. Don't let the exhilaration of skiing take away your concentration on how the ski *feels* and *reacts* to your commands. Try to be consistent with each pair of skis.

What to look for:

• How easily do the skis turn?
• Do they feel stable in the turn?
• Can I carve and hold the edges?
• Are they stable when riding flat?
• Do they ski well in different situations?
• How do they ski at slow and high speeds?
• How do they perform in soft and hard snow?

Boots

Some upscale shops, such as Pepi's in Vail, are moving toward allowing buyers to demo boots. This beats any other way to ensure comfort, fit and performance before buying.

Most retail stores offer a guaranteed-fit policy with the purchase of boots, which leaves the door open for returns. They allow three tries to work on a perfect fit before they take boots back. The third time is usually the charm.

To demo boots:

• Follow bootfitting procedures outlined in Chapter Five.
• Wear your custom footbeds and any other boot aids when testing.
• Get familiar with adjustment features and buckle systems.
• As with skis, establish a pattern of testing.

• Test for comfort, fit and performance. Pay attention to pressure points, whether your foot slides or slips anywhere in the boot (especially in the heel) and whether you can flex the cuff to control your skis. Notice lateral stiffness.

• *Always* demo boots with your own skis.

Chapter Summary:

In this chapter you learned about variances in price, quality and variety of rental packages; how, when and where to rent boots, skis and poles; and how to demo skis and boots.

Chapter Eight

Eyes on the thighs

"No, I don't do any regular exercising for skiing. Yes, I know I should."
— Jane, age 48, from Texas

"Skiing is exhausting. Being physically conditioned would help tremendously."
— Anonymous, age 47, from Colorado

S kiing is a sport you must be fit to do, not a sport you do to get fit. More and more, however, the ski industry glosses over the physical aspect of the sport by promoting it as "a total winter experience." Ski resorts refer to their ski mountains as products and market themselves to families as winter vacation destinations complete with sleigh rides, shopping and snowmobiling.

A ski vacation includes all of this, but we mustn't lose sight of the sport of skiing as, first and foremost, demanding physical exercise. People unprepared and ill-equipped, along with "couch potatoes" looking for fresh air, need to understand that they subject themselves to serious injury when they try to ski. It's a real bummer to fly home from a ski trip with X-rays of your bones instead of Kodak moments of your skiing. I've done it, and I can tell you crutches and stiff knee braces don't fit in commercial-airliner seats.

Injury remains the No. 1 fear experienced in skiing by men and women. Yet, in my survey, fewer than one-fourth of the women said they regularly perform any exercises to prevent injury. Many of the women in my survey said they do engage in physical activity, from walking to once-a-week tennis to aerobics, but most said they don't maintain a program for ski conditioning.

Pat Barbier, owner and director of the Vail Center for Physical Therapy in Vail, witnesses the results of failing to prepare. "The women we see in therapy [following injury] definitely lack physical conditioning for skiing," Barbier says. "We ask them what they did to get ready for skiing and they might say, 'I went biking last summer.'"

Many women don't realize that the right exercise can help them avoid ski injuries and improve performance. They simply didn't grow up understanding, as men did, the link between fitness, mental toughness and enjoyment. If they knew, I'm convinced more women skiers would be huffing and puffing, stretching and flexing, crunching and curling.

Orthopedic surgeon Laura Flawn, who also advises The University of Texas Lady Longhorns basketball team, believes physical fitness can prevent injury in every sport. As a skier, she also knows that sore muscles and tired legs can take the fun out of skiing. "When you're not fit you can't do the skills and skiing is not any fun," Flawn says. Her own fitness regime includes aerobics, weight training and running.

Many private fitness clubs offer ski-conditioning classes. But Herb Wetzel, who teaches these classes at the Athletic Club at Monaco, in Denver, estimates that women comprise only one-fourth of his students.

I'm not surprised. When I took the class a few years ago, the male teacher (not Wetzel), also happened to be a competition racquetball player. He geared the workout to match the strength and vigor of the majority of students in the class — strapping, *young*, male jocks. The gym oozed testosterone.

The pace wiped me out. After a few sessions, I opted for an exercise class taught by a woman. Although I found it more suited to women's stamina and strength, it wasn't targeted to skiers.

It's the same dilemma found in the aerobics industry by former heavyweight housewife-turned-fitness-maven Susan Powter: Overweight, unfit women looking for a beginning exercise program become turned off by aerobics classes filled with energetic, trim bodies bouncing around at a pace impossible for them to keep up.

No wonder when I talk to fitness instructors about teaching ski-conditioning classes for women, they contend that the demand isn't there.

One physical fitness teacher, Patty Wade, did find success in Aspen. Her classes are predominately women because her work-at-your-own-pace format allows gradual building of ski fitness levels. Wade's ski conditioning circuit has been captured on a video, *"In Shape to Ski"* (The Aspen Workout, $19.95).

There is more than one way for women to flex their skiing muscles. But before we get into a down-to-basics discussion on exercise, I'm going to tell you a story about one woman who learned in a single frightening encounter the power of training body and mind.

Empowerment

A man assaulted a tennis pal of mine from behind in the stairwell of a busy downtown parking garage when she was on her way to a luncheon. The attractive, slender woman, who stands 5 feet, 6 inches tall, was wearing a silk dress and 3-inch heels. Whirling around when the assailant grabbed her, she slammed her elbow into his chest. Face-to-face with the stranger — who she felt wanted more than her purse — she fought with such force that he finally gave up and ran.

Normally, this genteel woman admits, she could not have mustered the courage or strength to fight with a bigger, stronger man. But just before she drove downtown, she had worked out strenuously in an hour-long, individual tennis lesson, leaving her with an adrenaline high. By the time she encountered the stranger, it was a case of Wonder Woman meeting Peter Rabbit.

"My first instinct was *this guy is not going to get my jewelry!*" she recalls. "Then, with the mental image of hitting a big forehand still in my head, I pivoted and swung my arm back, thinking I would knock his head off with my racquet." My friend, by the way, has never taken a course in self-defense. "The ferociousness of my actions and the words out of my mouth were totally unlike me," she says. "I just felt invincible at that moment."

The woman police officer who responded told my friend that most women freeze in similar situations. The officer even admonished her for struggling, not knowing whether the attacker carried a weapon. Even though my friend explained her high energy level from the workout, the police officer didn't get it.

It's this kind of mental preparedness and empowerment derived from physical fitness that women need to be motivated in skiing. Authors John Naisbitt and Patricia Aburdene, in their best-selling book, "*Megatrends for Women,*" define empowerment as "feeling confident to act on your own authority." In the case of my friend in the parking-garage stairwell, she fought off an attacker because she believed she could. Feeling fit and strong gave her confidence and authority.

Cross training

Cultivating strong bones and muscles and maintaining a sound cardiovascular system should be goals in every woman's fitness program. How these goals are attained is a matter of preference. Women in my survey said they enjoy participating in other sports rather than taking regimented classes.

Dane Thomas, a Vail physical therapist and certified strength and conditioning specialist, believes in the power of motivation. "People are more easily motivated to do something that is beneficial and fun rather than something that is merely beneficial," he says. Thomas believes participating in other sports can be good ski training for recreational skiers with neither the time nor interest for fitness exercising. It's the anything-is-better-than-nothing theory. Be sure to seek qualified assistance whenever learning a new sport, he emphasizes.

Training should be frequent and consistent. He recommends a minimum of 20 minutes of sustained, elevated heart rate for aerobic activities at least three times a week. This means you don't start timing until you've reached your elevated heart-rate range. To achieve maximum benefit from your workout, go for the minimum 20 minutes, or longer, within this range.

To calculate your target heart rate:
- Subtract your age from 220.
- Multiply that number by .65 and then .85 to get the low and high parameters of your target heart-rate range.
- When you take your pulse immediately after exercising, you want the beats-per-minute reading to be between this range.
- Before beginning a new aerobic exercise, rest a few minutes until your pulse drops to a recovery rate of 120.

Risk factors should be figured into this formula. Primary risk factors include:
- being 45 years of age or older.
- blood pressure higher than 145/95.
- cigarette smoking.
- electrocardiogram abnormalities.
- diabetes mellitus.
- family history of coronary-artery disease younger than age 50.

If you fall into any of these categories, check with your doctor to determine your safe maximum heart rate.

Tops in cross training for skiing is in-line skating. Techniques and muscles used for in-line skating mimic those used in alpine skiing. Other good ski-training sports include mountain biking, running and road cycling.

These sports develop and maintain the physiological requirements for skiing: endurance, muscle strength, quickness, agility, flexibility, coordination and balance. They also develop mental fitness for skiing, including one's learning ability, confidence, visualization skills, the desire to succeed, and the motivation to overcome challenge. Last but certainly not least: They're *fun*.

Other sports activities good for skiers include water skiing, wind surfing, kayaking, rock and ice climbing, snowboarding, soccer, volleyball, racquet sports (tennis, racquetball, squash), basketball and motocross.

Yes, motocross. Racing dirt bikes is the cross-training sport Norwegian skier Stine Lise Hattestad took up to break through barriers she believed prevented her from edging out long-time rival Donna Weinbrecht in World Cup mogul competitions. She also added parachuting, rock climbing and barefoot water skiing to her training program. Her cross training paid off: Hattestad conquered her foe and her fear by winning the gold medal for mogul skiing in the 1994 Winter Olympic Games. TV viewers around the world shared her victory when, after winning, she relayed her secret: "I skied on the limit today," she said.

What about more feminine activities for ski conditioning, like aerobics and dance?

"Excellent exercise for skiing," says Lisa Feinberg Densmore, a ski racer on the Women's Pro Tour from 1984 to 1990 and a nationally recognized expert in fitness and skiing.

"I have used and taught aerobic workouts extensively for ski training because they incorporate all five areas of fitness," Densmore says. She believes the best aerobic exercise for skiers is a step workout: "I have been using step exercises and drills since the mid-1970s as a junior racer. Music keeps my tempo up and I have fun doing the choreography."

Densmore also believes ballet provides beneficial exercise routines for women skiers, increasing flexibility, toning, and balance. "Balance is the most critical skill for skiing," she says. "Ballet teaches you to have a strong center, while working your limbs independently." (Sound familiar?)

And when she learned that the entire Dartmouth College football team had enrolled in a ballet class, Densmore knew she was on the right track. "Although a few men take aerobics or dance, it's really a woman's domain," she says. "The guys don't know what they're missing. It could really help their skiing."

A varied fitness program incorporating cross-training sports, aerobics and dance will help you avoid mental and physical burnout. The best thing any woman can do for her skiing is to make physical activity a *lifestyle*. I don't know any women who ski well who don't also excel in other sports. Ski instructors who live near resorts bike, hike and kayak in summer months. Accomplished women skiers living in urban areas play tennis, ride bikes, run and do aerobics. To become a skier means to live an active, healthy life.

Bend zee knees, ouch!

A psychological boost also comes from knowing that you reduce risk of injury by building a strong, flexible body. Because knee injuries represent the most predominant ski injury in women, let's focus on knees.

In Chapter Two, we learned that the Q angle can cause women's knees to be dangerously out of alignment for skiing. While doctors know a woman's ligaments loosen during pregnancy (then recover following childbirth), some people believe women's ligaments naturally are looser than men's, although no scientific evidence supports this. It could be women's ligaments are just more fragile because muscles supporting them are less developed.

Physical therapist Thomas believes "the general density and size of the female ligament system leads them to be more susceptible to ligament injury." Combined with the Q angle, which puts more stress and higher forces on a woman's knees, it's as plain as your kneecap: Women — and women *skiers* in particular — are predisposed to knee injuries.

Experts say it's important for all skiers, perhaps more so for women, to strengthen *quadriceps and hamstrings*, which support the knees and maintain an appropriate strength ratio between the two muscle groups.

Quadriceps are four muscles extending down the front of the thigh and joining in a single tendon at the kneecap. These muscles straighten the knee and extend the lower leg. Hamstrings, a group of three muscles, run from the back of the hip bone to back of the knee, where they connect with the bones of the lower leg. It's the hamstrings that flex the knees. These two groups of muscles balance each other. Hamstrings reinforce the restraining function of the anterior cruciate ligament. Similarly, the quads support the posterior cruciate ligament and both reinforce functions of medial and lateral collateral ligaments.

"When the knee joint is subjected to a force," physical therapist Kacey Conway explains, "the muscles are the first line of defense. If the muscles are weak or fatigued, the next line of defense in an attack [injury] is the ligament." Clearly, muscle strength ranks as one of the most important factors in preventing knee ligament injury.

To compensate for the knock-knee tendency related to the Q angle, women need to develop their hip flexors and adductors — fancy names for the inner and outer thigh muscles. These muscles move the knees out and in. You use them to ride a horse and keep your knees from turning in while skiing. (Remember our dry-land drill in Chapter Two?)

If you're curious about your knee strength, most physical therapists, sports medicine clinics and rehabilitation centers use testing devices for finding out how you measure up. Ski area and ski town clinics use the devices to test ski patrollers and ski instructors, who are required to maintain muscle strength.

Strengthening muscles supporting the knees

Quadriceps

Health club workout:
(Fig. 2): The best machine for developing quads is the leg extension. Sitting comfortably in an upright position, place your feet under the round pads and slowly, five seconds each way, extend your legs to a locked or parallel position and then let them down.

Figure 2

Home workout:
(Fig. 3): Lunges are excellent for quads and buttocks. Holding hand weights at your sides for balance, take a "giant step" forward with your right leg and bend the knee until your thigh is parallel to the floor. Concentrate on lining up your

knee over your second toe, and do not extend the knee beyond the toes. Hold for five seconds. Repeat with the left leg.

Figure 3

You can also use the bottom step of a stairway, or a chair. From a standing position, place the toes of your right foot behind you on the step. With your left foot in front in the lunge position, knee lined up over toes as above, raise and lower your hips in a set of five. Repeat with the other leg.

Hamstrings
Health club workout:
(Fig. 4): The leg-curling machine is for hamstrings. Lie face down, flat on the bench with knees just over the edge. With your heels under the pads, slowly curl your legs back toward your buttocks until they are at a right angle, and then down. Again, count to five each way.

Figure 4

Home workout:

(Fig. 5): Lie flat on your back. Slide your knees up to about 45 degrees. Push on your heels to lift your hips as far off the ground as you can, pulling the abdominals down. Hold for as long as you can, then rest and repeat. This works both hamstrings at the same time.

Figure 5

Inner-thigh muscles

Health club workout:
(Fig. 6): Using the low pulley, stand with your back to the weights, strap attached to the left ankle, slightly bending the right leg. Bring the left leg behind the right; then, keeping it straight, bring it around in an arc ending in front of the standing leg. Repeat. Use light weights and lots of repetitions with each set.

Figure 6

Home workout:

Figure 7

(Fig. 7): Sit up with your back straight, hands around one bent knee. With the other knee slightly bent and to the outside, lift the leg up and down with the foot flexed. Repeat with the other leg. Add ankle weights for more strength.

Outer-thigh muscles

Health club workout:
(Fig. 8): Same as Fig. 6, except face the weights and begin with the working leg in front. End the arc behind the standing leg.

Figure 8

(Fig. 9): The leg-press machine is good for overall thigh muscle development. The athletic director at my club says women's knees tend to turn in when pushing on the foot rest. (Have you heard *that* before?) So, when extending your legs to press, strengthen your outer quads by maintaining alignment of knees over toes.

Figure 9

Figure 10

Home workout:
(Fig. 10): Lie on your left hip, propping up your side with your left elbow. Bend your knees to form a right angle with your torso. Lift the right leg about six inches parallel with the left, then lower. Without touching the bottom leg, lift again. Do a set, then repeat on the other side. You can also do this lying on your side with your hands between your knees, straight legs at a right angle to hips. Lift the upper leg with flexed foot as above, being careful not to turn your knee in. Ankle weights can be added here also.

Body Lines

This self-contained, portable exercise system uses resistance cords and is perfect for working the thighs and other skiing muscles. It's ideal for travel. Designed for U.S. Ski Team athletes as an alternate method of training on the road, Body Lines is now marketed to the public by Innovation Sports. The cords, ranging from around $55 to $70, can be ordered by calling (800) 222-4284.

Ski conditioning

Combining her ski-racing exercise program and favorite cross-training sports, Densmore produced a video to help skiers get ready for the slopes. In an informal, girl-next-door approach, *"BODY PREP! The Ultimate Ski Fitness Video"* (Driscoll Communications, $29.95) features Densmore and fellow pro-racers Leslie Baker-Brown and Laurie Baker-Wertz demonstrating how easy exercising in your own backyard can be. The video also shows how to intensify your training with the seasons and build toward winter.

I like the way the first part of the tape demonstrates how the exercises apply directly to skiing. In simultaneous sequences, the women perform dry-land exercises and cross-training sports; a smaller frame on the same screen features them skiing, illustrating how the exercises relate. The second segment shows a follow-along workout of aerobics, strength training and stretching.

Borrowing from *"BODY PREP!"* and the *U.S. Ski Team Training Manual*, here are suggestions for a ski-conditioning program to combine with the knee-strengthening exercises detailed earlier.

Five areas of fitness
Endurance

The ability to contract muscles against resistance over a long period of time is important. In skiing, good endurance will reduce fatigue and build energy. The following activities should be sustained at least 20 minutes to receive maximum endurance benefit:

- Hiking
- Running
- Biking
- Stationary biking
- Aerobics
- Treadmill or Stairmaster
- Rowing machine

Strength

Strengthening the muscles by progressively adding resistance is the most effective way to improve overall athletic ability. Without strong muscles in the legs, abdomen and arms, skiing is not as safe or enjoyable. Remember to breath properly during strength exercising. The two Xs work together: exhale on exertion. Heavy weights and fewer repetitions increase muscle; lighter weights and more repetitions will tone muscles without increasing mass. Do strength exercises every other day to allow muscles to recover.

Strength exercises include:
- Floor exercises for abdominals, arms and legs (detailed later in this chapter)
- Body Lines
- Weight machine/hand or free weights
- Rowing machine
- Water skiing
- Wind surfing

Quickness and Agility

The ability to change directions rapidly in a smooth, fluid manner is essential for skiing bumps and gates.

Good exercises include:
- Agility exercises
- Soccer
- Tennis
- Squash

Coordination and Balance

These are associated with agility and quickness, all excellent indicators of athletic ability. Balance is the overall skill required for skiing.

Good exercises include:
- Jumping rope
- In-line skating
- Kayaking
- All other sports

Flexibility

Before starting any activity, proper warm-up and stretching is most helpful for reducing the risk of injury. Physical therapist Thomas has seen it firsthand: "Flexibility cannot be stressed enough," Thomas says. "Without it, every activity will be compromised."

A skier whose muscles are flexible is less likely to tear or pull a muscle in a fall. Pre-stretched muscles allow greater strength and power for the workout. The *U.S. Ski Team Training Manual* suggests stretching after skiing to guard against muscle soreness and tightness.

Good exercises for enhancing flexibility include:
- Stretching exercises (detailed later in this chapter)
- Dance

Floor exercises

Perform each exercise one to three times, depending on your fitness level. Do each for 15 to 30 seconds, rest for the same amount of time, then repeat. Rest two to five minutes between each exercise.

• **Lateral thrust** (Fig. 11): Explosively jump from side to side from one foot to the other. Develops quads and simulates side-to-side motion of the legs in skiing.

Figure 11

• **Stomach cramp** (Fig. 12): Lie on your back, knees bent and feet crossed in the air. With hands behind the head, slowly curl up and touch elbows to knees; then do a set crossing right elbow to left knee and alternate. Works the abdominal muscles, one of the most neglected muscle groups in fitness and one of the most important for skiing.

A strong stomach helps you recover when you sit back and helps maintain upper body control while the feet work independently.

• **Push-up** (Fig. 13): With your back straight, lower chest to the floor and up. To make this exercise a little easier, drop knees to the ground. Increases arm strength needed for carrying ski equipment and getting up after falls.

Figure 13

• **Bouncing tuck** (Fig. 14): In a tuck position like downhill racers, bounce by lifting feet off the floor. Start high and drop to a lower tuck. Develops quadriceps and hamstrings in the legs. These muscle groups should maintain equal strength and are important in all levels of skiing.

Figure 14

Figure 15

• **Stomach crunch** (Fig. 15): Lie on your back, hands behind the head, curl upper body as you raise your knees; then extend legs and lower upper body, not letting feet or head touch the floor. More work on the all-important midsection of the body. A strong stomach means a stable back.

• **Arm dip** (Fig. 16): Supporting yourself between two chairs, firmly grip the chair backs and raise your body until your feet leave the floor. Then, slowly lower yourself until your feet contact the floor again. Strong arms help with race starts and poling on catwalks.

Figure 16

• **One-leg knee bend** (Fig. 17): Stand on one leg with the other extended out and knee bent; slowly lower the standing leg, making sure not to go below 90 degrees. If you have knee problems, don't go as low. For easier balancing, use a chair for

Figure 17

support. Uses the same leg-muscle control as weighting and releasing a ski.

• **Sit-up** (Fig. 18): With knees bent and your lower back on the floor, slowly curl torso up, elbows to knees. A strong stomach means a strong back and helps prevent lower back pain after skiing.

Figure 18

• **Side push-up** (Fig. 19): Lie on your right side, right hand on left side of waist, left hand on floor in front of right shoulder; extend left arm, raising torso off floor and then lower. A sturdy upper body will help direct the hands forward and up, creating a solid pole plant.

Figure 19

• **Squat thrust** (Fig. 20): Start with hands on the floor slightly ahead of your feet; kick feet back to push-up position, then return to squat; make an explosive jump up and land in the next squat. Creates the muscle power needed to ski dynamically and aggressively and to handle faster speeds.

Figure 20

Agility exercises

The goal of these exercises is to gain the ability to move quickly under any circumstances.

Figure 21   Figure 22

- **Carioca** (Fig. 21): Lateral running, crossing left leg in front of right, right in front of left, in a line. Develops quick feet.
- **Bench hops** (Fig. 22): Hop quickly from side to side over a low bench or pillow with feet together, hands forward. Start with 10, build to 20. Helps you feel quicker from ski to ski, especially when making jump turns on steeps.
- **Step-ups:** Using a variety of patterns, step up and down the bottom step of a stairway as fast as you can. Helps with making snappy, short turns down the fall line.
- **Backward run:** Stay low, pumping shoulders and arms while backpedaling in different directions. Keep the upper torso quiet — no hip mobility. Develops independent footwork.

Flexibility exercises

Each of these positions should be held for 20 seconds, creating the sensation of mild stretching in the muscles. Do not bounce through the stretch; breathe normally. *Do not stretch until you have done a thorough warm-up.* Exercise trainer Karen Stubbs warns: "You need to get the body temperature up and blood pumping. Warm muscles are more pliant than cold muscles, which are in a contracted state. If you try to stretch a contracted muscle, you may feel it in the tendons and ligaments, which need to be tight to hold the joints in place." When skiing, take a warm-up run first, then stretch.

- **Side stretch:** With legs apart, grab your wrist overhead with one hand and gently pull to the side, stretching the upper back and shoulders.

• **Toe touch:** With feet shoulder-width apart and soft, not rigid, knees, bend down and touch your toes, feeling a stretch in the hamstrings.

• **Standing quad stretch** (Fig. 23): Balance on one foot, grab the other by the top of the foot behind you and bend forward at the waist, stretching the quad to balance the stretch of the hamstring.

Figure 23

• **Lunge stretch** (Fig 24): With both hands on the floor in front of you parallel to your left foot, extend your right leg back, bending the left leg at a right angle, taking care to keep the knee at a right angle over the foot. Repeat on the other side. This stretches the groin, hamstrings, quads and hips.

Figure 24

• **Leg crossover** (Fig. 25): Sitting on the floor, cross your right leg over your left knee. Place your left elbow to the outside of your right knee and look over your left shoulder. Repeat on the other side. Feel a stretch in your lower back and hips.

Figure 25

• **Calf stretch** (Fig. 26): Lean hands against a wall. With toes pointed straight ahead, extend one leg behind you and feel a stretch in the calf and Achilles' tendon. Repeat on the other leg. Make sure your heels stay flat.

Figure 26

Move it on the mountain

After your first run of the day, when your blood is flowing fast and your muscles are warm, do these stretching exercises:

- **Torso twist**: Keeping your hips quiet, swing your arms from side to side, giving your upper body, shoulders and arms a good stretch.
- **T-stretch**: Bracing yourself with ski poles, lift your leg so the tail of the ski is perpendicular to the ground in front of you and your extended leg is parallel to the ground. Feel a stretch in your hamstrings.
- **Tip-drop stretch**: Do the reverse, placing the tip of the ski on the snow behind you, stretching the quads.
- **Side Lunges**: Bend the left leg as you slide the right leg as far as you can to the side and back. This stretches quads, hamstrings and groin.
- **Calf Stretch**: Leaning on your ski poles, slide one leg back until you feel a stretch in the calf.

Do neck rolls, side stretches and toe touches in your skis. If you have lower-back pain when you ski, tuck your ski poles in the small of your back and lean on them, gently stretching through the mid-section when you're standing in the lift line.

Whatever you choose for your ski conditioning regime, make sure you include plenty of aerobics for your heart and lungs and exercises for the specific muscles used in skiing.

Make home exercises a part of your day. I do mine while catching up on the TV morning news. I also do leg lifts, knee bends and stretching while I'm on the phone. Focus on keeping your knees over your toes throughout the day while climbing stairs, sitting, even standing. Contract your inner thigh muscles while you "squeeze a dime" with your butt muscles. You'll create new muscle memory that you'll notice on the slopes!

What if ...?

If you are injured while skiing, play it safe and visit the medical clinic. Jack Mason, director of the ski patrol at Winter Park, has observed many injured women over the years. He believes women tolerate more pain than men. "If you don't believe that, you've never had a baby," Mason jokes.

Do not ignore pain. Women who have given birth and post-menopausal women (because of osteoporosis), in particular, can sustain pelvis fractures from falling hard on their butts. Because the pelvis houses the bladder and other vital organs, the danger of not being treated lies in bone fragments piercing your innards. So save the toughness for childbirth. On the slopes, be sensible when it hurts: Reach out and tell somebody.

Carry a credit card when you ski. Most ski-area clinics are not set up for billing health insurers. If you're younger than 18, you'll also need a parental permission slip for treatment.

On being sensible, Mason shared an interesting statistic: He says 87 percent of people killed by lightning are men. Does this tell us that more men play golf, or that more men don't know enough to come in out of the rain?

Chapter Summary:
We emphasized that skiing is a sport you must be fit to do, not do to get fit. You risk injury and

enjoyment when you are not physically and mentally prepared.

A good fitness program includes cross-training sports as well as exercises for specific muscle groups used in skiing; in particular, for women, the muscles supporting the knees because of the Q angle.

You learned to calculate your target heart rate and how to exercise in order to develop and maintain the physiological requirements for skiing: endurance, muscle strength, quickness and agility, flexibility, coordination and balance.

Recommended viewing:
"BODY PREP! The Ultimate Ski Fitness Video." To order, write to Driscoll Communications and Densmore Associates, 45 Lyme Road, Suite 206-A, Hanover, NH 03755, or call (800) 424-0033.
"In Shape to Ski." To order write to The Aspen Workout, P.O. Box 1305, Aspen, CO 81612, or call (800) 925-9754.

Chapter Nine

Fear less

"I'm terrified of getting on a slope I can't ski and not being able to get down."
— *LeAnn, age 35 from Texas*

"Fear of injury and speed keep me from skiing as well as I'd like ... Skiing more and getting over some simple fears would greatly improve my skiing. I would like to ski down moguls, knees together, with a smile on my face."
— *Anonymous, age 40 from Oklahoma*

"I don't know if an inner fear holds me back or if I just don't care enough. I guess it will take the right person, not only to teach me to ski, but to help me overcome the fear (or whatever it is)."
— *Maureen, age 53 from Colorado*

Mary Jo has skied off and on for 34 of her 54 years. She loves everything about the sport and enjoys ski vacations with family, even though they long ago surpassed her in ability. Mary Jo's biggest drawback: paralyzing fear of getting hurt.

Sometime she finds herself on terrain beyond her capabilities. "I am in *agony*," she says. "I try to avoid being in these spots because I know I'm not going to feel good about myself. Consequently, I haven't fallen in 20 years. But I haven't gotten off the green slopes, either!"

Still, Mary Jo has had fun on the slopes over the years. She remembers three occasions when she even skied without fear. Each time immediately followed a traumatic episode in her life: the Cesarean birth of her daughter, her own open-heart surgery, and the removal of her wisdom teeth.

"In my mind, I said, 'If I can go through this, I can do anything,'" Mary Jo recalls. "And I skied better than I've ever skied."

But the little positive voice turned negative again and the petrifying fear returned.

Now, however, Mary Jo is putting into practice two new tricks to manage fear. "I indulge in a Bloody Mary before I go out, and then I ski to Placido Domingo and John Denver on tape when I want to get through the rough parts," she says, laughing.

The feeling of being paralyzed with fear atop a ski run is familiar to anyone in a high-risk sport like skiing, especially anyone still learning. Your stomach agitates like the rinse cycle of a washing machine, your knees and hands shake, your heart pounds. You lose whatever motivation got you there in the first place.

I remember a time in 1963 when I froze atop Bradley's Bash at Winter Park. My late husband, a ski racer when he was in high school and college, was encouraging me to ski more difficult runs. Looking down that steep, wavy trail blanketed with fresh snow (this was in the days before grooming), I was terror-stricken. The longer I stood there, the steeper and bumpier the run became. I could not get my legs to turn. I couldn't move forward in a traverse, let alone go down. A kick-turn in my shaky state was out of the question.

Finally, after much coaxing and cajoling, I took my skis off and slid down, embarrassed to tears. The next day, I signed up for a lesson.

In their book, *"Inner Skiing"* (Random House, $4.99 for revised paperback), learning expert Timothy Gallwey and psychologist Bob Kriegel describe two types of fear:

- Fear I is the paralyzing fear that interferes with our ability to perform at our best.
- Fear II is the body's natural response to challenge, the fight-or-flight response. In emergencies, mothers react instinctively to protect children from harm. This good fear heightens perception and provides energy to move beyond normal capabilities.

Fear I, the type we mostly feel in skiing, has three essential components:

- The sense of *danger.*
- The sense of *vulnerability* – you can get hurt by this danger.
- The sense of *inability to overcome* the danger.

If any one of these ingredients is missing, Gallway and Kriegel maintain, no real fear exists.

They explain: In skiing, the slope usually is perceived as the danger and the skier as vulnerable. But if the skier feels competent to ski the trail, no fear exists. Likewise, if the skier is incompetent but the hill is too flat to be perceived as a danger, no fear exists. Lastly, if the skier feels no vulnerability to being hurt (hard to imagine) no fear exists.

The solution to coping with fear: increasing awareness of the realities of a given situation — that is, learning to perceive *real* danger, to know one's competence and one's *actual* vulnerability.

Though some people feel less fear, no one is immune to it. Even the best skiers in the world don't escape fear. Following her gold-medal-winning Super G run in the 1994 Olympic Winter Games, U.S. Olympic Team member Diann Roffe-Steinrotter said she was "so nervous at the start I almost lost my stomach."

Teammate Picabo Street, who won a silver medal in those Games, said the memory of Austrian downhiller Ulrike Maier's death on the race course two weeks earlier was "all over the faces of the women here [at Lillehammer]. It's right on the surface. I look at it as God's way of looking down at all of us and saying, 'Watch out; be careful.'"

Dealing with fear

In skiing, learning to recognize, understand and manage fear will go a long way toward enhancing performance and enjoyment. Realize that every skier, regardless of ability, deals with fear. Said Roffe-Steinrotter of her winning run: "I just let my instincts go. I said, 'I can do this.' Then I relaxed and had fun."

Another Olympic competitor tries to think about task-specific things in her skiing to take her mind off the bigger picture, which is "scared to death!" she says.

Asked about the danger of fast skiing, Olympic skier Street says she uses her head to manage fear. "I try not to think about it," Street says. "When it hits me, I am able to pull back a little bit."

Pulling back is the No. 1 tactic cited by most of the women who participated in my survey. They admitted to skiing cautiously, skiing slower and skiing more in control when they find themselves on terrain that freaks them out. Others said they work on improving their skills with lessons.

Women are less fearful skiing with instructors or people they trust — an important aspect of exploring new or more challenging terrain. One woman who participated in my survey said when she doesn't feel safe, "Sometimes I cry and swear I'll never go back. But somehow I 'get it' and get down. It's not pretty!"

Still, many others completely avoid anything that sends shivers down their spines. In some cases, this is smart — like the woman afraid of being hit by a reckless or out-of-control skier. She restricts her skiing to weekdays and uncrowded runs.

But sometimes avoidance can become self-defeating. For anyone wanting to improve skiing technique, small risks on more difficult runs are necessary. An example: the woman who says skiing in the trees scares her. She still skis in them, but slowly rather than not at all.

Drawing the line at skiing certain types of threatening trails comes easy for some women. After all, skiing is supposed to be enjoyable and rewarding. Not everyone thinks challenge is fun. "I am happy skiing with my family for recreation and fun," says Jean, another survey participant, who skis five times a year or so. Those skiers who are not willing to risk a little prefer to save anxious moments for the inevitable poor conditions like flat light, blizzards and ice.

A few women in the survey said they feel no fear at all about skiing. An intermediate skier from Tennessee swore that if she had any fear, she wouldn't ski!

Fear of injury is the overriding concern for women (and men) in skiing. Situations women in my survey said they fear most: losing control, hitting an object, such as a tree, careening over "the edge," and getting stuck on a trail beyond their abilities.

It's finding themselves on a too-difficult trail that intermediate-level women said they fear most. Though mentioned a few times by my survey respondents, fear of failure and not keeping up ranked low on the list.

The most dreaded snow condition among women is ice. The most terrifying terrain is a mogul field. And steep or icy moguls really blows them away. Consequently, what most women in my survey said they wanted to improve was bump technique.

Others worry about other things. "My greatest fear is not having fun," says 24-year-old Christie, who skis nine times a year. Her solution: "Dress warm, go with cool people, and don't ski on holiday weekends (especially in California!)."

Annette, 29, said she worries about someone running into her. "It happens a lot in the East at small ski resorts that are overpacked," she said. To overcome it, she fights for her space. "I ski aggressively, and when it happens, I preach to them and turn them in."

The best way to avoid being hit is to ski in your "corridor." I like to pretend I'm in an alley about as wide as a highway lane. If you learn to make short, quick turns down the alley's fall line, you can stay on the side of the slope, away from the maddening crowd. The snow is usually better there, too.

I was surprised that most of the beginner and expert woman skiers in my survey said they dealt with fear in the same way — improving technique. Advanced skiers, meanwhile, said they were more likely to use caution and ski within their abilities than to take lessons or practice skills to get through intimidating situations. Skiing slow and in control ranked first with intermediates. The second-rated choice, intermediates said, was that they would just as soon avoid harder terrain than figure out how to tackle it.

For me, practicing skills and focusing on technique prove best for coping with fear in skiing.

Pushing through fear

In her book, *"Feel the Fear and Do It Anyway"* (Ballantine Books, $12), psychologist Susan Jeffers lists five truths about fear that I have learned to apply to my skiing:

• The fear will never go away as long as I continue to grow [in my skiing].

• The only way to get rid of the fear of doing something [skiing bumps] is to go out and ... do it [ski bumps].

- The only way to feel better about myself is to go out ... and do it [ski bumps].
- Not only am I going to experience fear whenever I'm on unfamiliar territory, but so is everyone else [of my ability].
- Pushing through fear is less frightening than living with the underlying fear that comes from feeling helpless [being immobilized on a slope].

My daughter, Susan, credits her ability to push through fear in skiing to a time when she was 9 years old skiing with the family at Steamboat. Accidentally, we landed on a steep, no-way-out bump run called Cyclone. Crying, Susan sat down at the top and refused to move. Her father knew she was capable of skiing it. "You can sit here and cry until tears freeze to your face or ski down," he told her, matter-of-factly. "There's no other way. You can do it. Bye!"

He and I followed the boys — who by then were long gone — down the first part of the run. When we looked back, Susan carefully was criss-crossing the hill, focusing on her turns, determined not to fall. She didn't.

"All of a sudden, being left behind seemed more scary than going down," Susan recalls. "I had to do it."

Turn fear into energy

Instead of working to eliminate fear, learn to turn it into energy. In their clinics on skiing the extreme, brothers Rob and Eric DesLauriers and Dan and John Egan teach life-saving tactics prompted by the fight-or-flight response. They show how to avoid a sudden cliff or tree when skiing powder by throwing your feet and skis up as if you were jumping into a swimming pool.

This maneuver will stop you in your tracks and could save your life.

Men in the clinics catch on easily. But when I did it, it took me several tries before I got comfortable catapulting my body at will. Men learn this early in life — diving for a pass or tackling in football, flinging their bodies on the ground to pop-up a volleyball, or sliding into first base. Some women gymnasts do it, but theirs is a more controlled aerial, not an indiscriminate throwing the body!

Recently, I participated in Women's Week in Telluride. As part of the "extend-your-boundary" philosophy behind the women-teaching-women ski clinics, an optional activity was offered to the group: climbing the wall.

After watching my sons scale indoor climbing walls over the years, muscles bulging as their arms strain to reach the next handhold, I never thought I'd do that one day. Yet, by the fourth day of skiing in a supportive environment led by such vibrant women, I felt exceptionally strong and capable, physically and mentally. Next thing I knew, I was hugging a wall 30 feet above the ground. My spirits soared even higher! I had entered a new comfort zone. I was fearless! The first thing I did when I got home? Told my sons!

New skills for conquering fear

Here's an example of how the Woman's Ski Discovery program at Vermont's Sugarbush Resort helps alleviate fear in women skiers. Ashley

Fischer and Nancy Luke, program directors; Patricia Simmons, a psychiatrist; and psychologists Barbara Kester and Peggy Sax wrote this explanation for *"WomenSki"*:

Women seem to experience fear more often and more intensely than men. It occurs at all levels and for many reasons.

It is important to understand the difference between appropriate fear and inappropriate fear. Fear can be appropriate when it gives us proper respect for the task at hand and protects us from doing something dangerous. Fear can also be disproportionate and interfere with performance. It can paralyze us or drive us away from a situation that might have been quite safe, even fun.

A novice skier may be afraid of speed. An advanced skier may be just as afraid of bumps. Adverse conditions scare some. Terrain may scare others. Some are afraid of wind, some of heights, some of powder. Almost everyone is afraid of being hurt. We have yet to meet a woman who is unafraid of losing control.

We don't have control over weather or conditions, and the terrain is laid out for us. However, we do have the skill to gain or regain control. Through skill development and positive psychological training, we can learn to look at each threatening situation that presents itself and, rather than panic or respond in an inappropriate manner, say to ourselves, "I can do this. What skills and attitude do I need to accomplish the task?" Through repetition and continued success, our responses will become more and more automatic. We can learn to trust our skills and ourselves. We can allow realistic fear to guide us while inappropriate fear lessens, even disappears.

Skill development

First and foremost, everyone from the never-ever to the advanced skier needs the appropriate skills. Everybody benefits from proper coaching. The broader our repertoire of technical skills, the greater number of challenges we can meet with confidence. While other chapters in *"WomenSki"* deal more specifically with the technical aspects of skiing, in this section we will focus on helping women choose the skills they might want to use in fear-producing situations and framing our teaching in a way that develops confidence and minimizes anxiety.

Language and imagery

Traditional ski teaching often teaches skills in a way that isn't comforting to most women. How many of us have been told to "launch ourselves down the hill" when initiating a turn? How many of us have had our lack of aggressiveness thrown in our faces? Even the term fall line contains negative connotations.

We teach skiers to become more masterful, not necessarily aggressive. Instead of fall line, we say *flow line*, a more accurate term describing what we want to do. Wouldn't you rather *flow* down the hill than *fall* down it? Our skiers are not told to *launch* their bodies down the hill. Instead, one of our participants imagines Mel Gibson is standing downhill from her and she rises across her skis to embrace him. Which do you find more appealing?

Non-threatening terrain

Not only do we use less threatening language and imagery, we also introduce new skills and concepts on less threatening terrain. It is important to remember you will be less likely to experiment with something new if you are concerned about the terrain. We only need one challenge at a time. An important component of learning to ski is trust — trust in the instructor, trust in the new skill, and most of all, trust in ourselves and our abilities. Trusting is difficult if we're afraid before we begin. There is plenty of time to practice new skills in the real world after we have begun to understand and feel them in our skiing.

Massage the comfort zone

Another way to create a more positive learning environment is to retain your old skills. You have been getting down the hill in a way that works for you. We may modify your movement pattern and enhance certain skills or de-emphasize others, but we want you to keep everything else (unless it is completely counterproductive). The bigger your bag of tricks, the more versatile you can be and the better you can cope in an uncomfortable situation. Everyone has occasions to be happy they know how to snowplow. And the side-slip can be incredibly useful in difficult sections. We don't want to lose these skills just because we now know how to make a parallel turn. These skills can keep us out of trouble. (*Survival skills* are discussed later in this section.)

It is important to keep challenging yourself by moving in and out of your comfort zone. If you don't, your zone will get smaller and smaller until you have regressed and feel anxious about everything. You will never improve or learn to use your new skills if you don't keep moving, physically and emotionally. We don't advocate throwing yourself out of your comfort zone. This can promote anxiety and fear. We like to think of massaging its barriers. Ease yourself in and out. When you leave it, return to it on the next run.

Psychological techniques

As important as technical-skill development is, we also need to learn to manage our fear. The most skilled skier can forget everything in a moment of fear. Unfortunately, that is usually when we most need to tap into the technical survival skills that are going to get us out of the dilemma. We need to empower ourselves to accomplish the task.

Make good choices

First and foremost, it is important to make appropriate choices, to know what you can and can't handle. It is also important to learn to say no when peers (often males) ask you to ski something you know is beyond your ability. Learn to choose an alternate route, meet them later and continue to feel good about yourself. When you do make the choice to follow them, which may mean leaving your comfort zone, learn to listen to yourself. You might prefer the challenge early in the day when you feel fresh, not late in the afternoon when you're exhausted. Challenge yourself if and when you want, not because you — or someone else — feel you have to. The choice should be yours.

There are times when you find yourself in a state of fear. The weather conditions may have changed. You misread the trail map. Someone told you a trail was groomed and it was all bumps. A well-meaning friend took you to a run you can't handle. By training yourself to take control, you can trust your own ability and ski to safety.

Relax

One of the first techniques we teach is *Progressive Relaxation.* First we establish a general state of relaxation before we go out on the hill. This is done by systematically tensing specific muscle groups, holding that tension and then relaxing those muscles as we feel the tension flow out through the extremities. Tension and contraction alternate with release.

"Letting go" is extremely important in maintaining flow and rhythm in our skiing. Try one right now. Make a fist and tighten the arm muscles throughout the forearm right up through the biceps. Now, hold that tension for 30 seconds. Take a deep breath and allow everything to relax. Feel the tension flow right out through your fingertips? Repeat with the other arm.

You can then move through the whole body, shoulders, trunk, legs and feet. For maximum effect, try it with relaxing music. You should feel much more relaxed and open. As you get more practiced, you can start associating a word or sound with the state of relaxation. Ideally, you will learn to invoke this relaxed state by calling up your word whenever you find yourself in a fear-producing situation.

You can also do a mini relaxation on the chair lift, or right on the hill, whenever you start to feel anxious. As you get more adept at recognizing where you carry your tension, you can isolate that part of the body and relax only it.

How often do you scrunch up your toes when you hit ice? It's as though you are trying to hold on to the surface with your toes, right through your ski boots! All you gain is pain. You probably never developed skills for skiing on ice because you wasted energy holding on for dear life. Next time you find yourself on an icy slope, try stopping and squeezing your toes. Hold that tension and feel it. Take a deep breath and allow the tension to flow out the bottom of your feet, relaxing them in your boots. Start again and see if you and your feet aren't more relaxed for the rest of the run.

Imagery

Women's Ski Discovery also uses imagery to enhance learning and control fear. When you are skiing on a crowded slope, imagine a white light emanating from your center and enveloping you. Nobody can penetrate that light, so you can keep skiing down the hill in its protection. In the moguls, think of your ski tips as playful dolphins. Imagine how dolphins ride the swells. They plunge, they jump, they cavort. Most important, their flexible bodies undulate up and around, in and out of the waves, just as your skis can in the bumps.

Progressive relaxation combined with visual imagery is an even more powerful tool for dealing with fear. In a relaxed state, you can learn to introduce vivid images of yourself skiing. You can create your own drama as rich and as detailed as your imagination will allow. Sports psychologists and professional athletes most often use imagery to enhance performance. We have found it helps women gripped by fear or apprehension to create alternate scripts. Imagine yourself gliding freely down a favorite trail rather than careening out of control. Some women picture themselves skiing confidently down the same trail where they once experienced a frightening fall or an injury. What you see is what you get. A positive inner image and expectation will lead to a positive experience on the slopes.

Reframing attitude

Most women need some attitude adjustment. If they make 10 good turns and five of those felt good, we ask them if they remember the five good ones or five bad ones. Almost every woman remembers the bad ones. Women approach fearful situations the same way. We teach them to *reframe* negative attitudes and look at themselves in a positive light to take control of the situation.

On a basic level, how do you view the mountain? Do you see it as an adversary or as a partner? Do you fight the mountain, holding on to each turn, leaning up the hill, not allowing gravity to help you? Instead of thinking in terms of "woman vs. mountain," reframe that attitude to "woman and mountain." Look at the view. Enjoy being outdoors. You have spent a great deal of money to have a good time with this mountain. Use your skills to let gravity start to pull you into your turns so that you can let go and float down the hill, one turn flowing into the next. Suddenly, you're dancing down instead of struggling. You are in harmony with your surroundings, not in conflict.

Now, start to reframe other attitudes. How about viewing fear as respect? *You don't ski slowly — you have excellent speed control.* Good speed control allows you to carry more speed with less apprehension. *You are not a wimp — you exercise good judgment.* When you trust your judgment, you explore new horizons. You can even resort to humor: Ice becomes "loud powder." Hard snow chunks become "death cookies." Humor doesn't make the problem disappear but it allows us to put it in perspective and settle on a strategy.

Positive alternate response

Finally, when confronted by a fear-producing situation, we need to replace a useless panic response with a *positive alternate response.* The more we rely on the appropriate positive-alternate response, the more automatic its use will become. Eventually the fear will disappear.

If you are on a trail with trees, try looking between and around the trees, not at them. How many times have you focused on an ice patch and then found yourself on top of it? Next time, try looking for the good snow instead. Confronted by a steep section of the trail, look at the flats beyond. It's a much more comforting focus and you'll find, in a few turns, that you've reached those flats. Look at the bumps as a series of opportunities to turn, rather than a minefield. You know you can make turns, so look for the paths and go at your own pace. It may not always be a pretty sight, but you will get down!

Survival skills

Our survival skills provide excellent positive-alternate responses. In Women's Ski Discovery, we teach key words to help us tap into those survival skills in times of stress.

For example, as many of us approach ice, our mind screams, "Ice!" Our downhill arm flies up in the air and our skis slide out from under us. Instead, try this. As you are sliding over the ice looking for good snow, fully extend your downhill arm in front of you and lower it to the ground. This will help you balance over your more stable downhill ski. It also helps you keep your center over your feet so your weight doesn't get back, allowing your skis to shoot out from under you.

This stabilizing movement lets you focus on the safe haven of soft snow ahead and sustain movement down the hill. You'll slide over that icy surface and reach the safety of good snow.

Give that positive-alternate response a name. We simply use "arm." Before you know it, with practice and repeated success, ice will be replaced with arm and you will begin to feel a mastery over this extremely threatening situation.

What about steeps? We have a survival skill we call "tips up the hill" — steering our inside ski up the hill to decelerate at the end of each turn. You can call on this to control speed right from the start instead of invoking the power panic turn after you lose control.

Instead of leaning up the hill, holding each turn and struggling down, reach down the hill, with each pole touch. This will allow your energy to flow in the right direction. Don't forget: the sooner and more efficiently you start your turn, the more time you'll have to finish it. It's in the finish portion of the turn where we gain control. When you hold back out of fear, your weight drops back, your skis get away from you and you lose control. Replace holding back with contact with the front of your boots. This way, you can make an immediate adjustment before things get away from you.

As you become more proficient and gain more technical knowledge, you will create your own "positive-alternate responses" uniquely useful to you. You will learn to anticipate situations that provoke fear or panic. You will also learn to respond in a positive, take-charge manner; or at least you will head off a counter-productive reaction. At best, fear may disappear altogether.

Fear — both appropriate and inappropriate — can be managed effectively on the slopes. These techniques, combined with skill development, will help you learn a sense of well-being, confidence and mastery. If we know we can control our own destiny, we can let go of inappropriate fear. It can become a thing of the past. Without fear, we can really have fun and rediscover the joy of skiing. And we can look at our accomplishments and feel justified pride.

Fantastic & familiar

Two "F-words" allow me to ski where it's scary — *fantastic* and *familiarity*. I will try new terrain, technique or higher speeds when conditions are fantastic — a 9 or 10 on my 1-to-10 scale of the perfect ski day.

One day in early spring at Blackcomb in the Canadian Rockies, daffodils were blooming in the village, new snow felt as soft as rabbit's fur and the royal blue sky dazzled. The temperature, warm for skiing, hovered around 40 and the sun defined every variation in the snow. My skis were perfectly tuned and ideal for the conditions. Because I trusted the surface and my equipment, I had a confidence, almost a cockiness, in my skiing. I was boogying. Nothing to think about except lovin' life!

About midday, when I was skiing with a male friend, we stopped where a crowd of skiers was peering over a ravine. With the same spirit that propelled me all morning, I slipped over the side, methodically making one turn after another down the steep center, until I reached the runout. A good, solid run. At the bottom, I waited and waited for my friend. Twenty, 30 minutes passed.

"I couldn't make that first turn," he said when he finally showed up, the fear plain on his face.

Later, when I heard people bragging about skiing "the Saudan" (Saudan Couloir, a double black diamond chute named after the French extreme skier Sylvian Saudan), I realized how lucky I was to have hit it on one of my fearless days!

Familiarity is easy to understand: You move more freely in the darkened bedroom of your home, where you're familiar with the furnishings, than in a pitch-black hotel room, where moving too fast might cause you to stub your toe. In skiing, you can be more gutsy on a run you've previously skied or on the kind of terrain or snow you've already experienced.

At Mammoth Mountain in California, I had to be coaxed by a patient guide into jumping off a cornice for the first time. The only way to get from where I was to where he stood was to (gulp!) get air, just as he did. I had no choice, he said. Heart pounding, hands shaking, I sucked up my knees and flew. It was so much fun, I went back again and again, each time with less fear. The more familiar it became, the more I expanded my comfort zone. Experts call this desensitization.

The same thing happened with my fear of steeps. After hiking up to and skiing down McConkey's Bowl, a precipitous drop off Jupiter Peak at Park City, Utah, I finally "got it": The feeling of letting go of a good edge set, reaching forward for my pole plant and projecting my body down the fall line. Now, whenever I ski steep runs — my favorite type of terrain — I call on those sensations and say to myself, "I know how to do this. I've done this."

It's like riding a bike — scary at first, but with practice you master the technique and dispel your fears. Learning to ski the right way, plus mileage, mileage, mileage, will do wonders for your courage.

Still, occasional fear may seep in. When my youngest son, Nick, was 17, he and I broke trail in the trees on the steep North Face of Peak 9 at Breckenridge, unable to find the run we had set out to ski. We came to a chute no wider than a tall slide in a children's playground and about as long. Nick breezed down it, but I froze.

Though not nearly as steep as other runs I'd skied, its narrow boundaries, flanked by thick trees, made me feel confined. While the chute fanned a little at the bottom, I knew I'd have to make a quick turn to avoid trees. The longer I looked at it, the more nervous I got. I opted to go around in untracked powder rather than slide down that little blip of a hill!

Chapter Summary:
This chapter shows us fear is universal. Learning to recognize, understand and deal with the paralyzing fear we feel on the slopes can help us ski better and enjoy it more.

You learned about fear-managing tactics from authors, other women skiers, Olympic racers, and instructors and psychologists who teach the women's ski seminar at Sugarbush, Vermont.

For information:
Women's Ski Discovery: write to Sugarbush Resort, RR1 Box 350, Warren, VT 05674-9993; or call (800) 53-SUGAR, (800) 537-8427.

Chapter Ten

Lady, it's cold outside

"I dislike skiing when it's soooo cold!"
— *Traci, age 26 from Colorado*

"What I dislike about skiing is trying to find attractive, functional, properly fitting ski clothes."
— *Christine, age 44 from Colorado*

If "a women is what a woman wears" applied to ski clothes, we all could become technically correct just by slipping into something more comfortable!

Do you know what ceramics, soda pop bottles, zirconium carbide and insects have in common? They're all sources of materials that go into your ski clothes.

The list of state-of-the-art fabrics and fibers that make up ski clothes reads like a chemistry book. Today's technical threads move moisture, block wind, shed water, wick vapor, trap air, transport perspiration, heat up, cool down and breathe. They do everything but carve turns.

Warmth, comfort and a pocket where you need it are the hallmarks of ski clothing of the 90s. Think of it as equipment.

Although department-store jackets may look and feel like those you see on ski slopes, look closer. Read hangtags. If you want real warmth, you want the latest technology from companies that make clothing specifically for cold-weather sports.

Taking a cue from equipment makers, ski clothing designers listened to women who said they want function with their fashion. **Hard Corps Sports** reflects the clothing side of skiing's gender revolution. When Hard Corps started in 1984, its male-only line was designed to keep the serious skier comfortable, warm and dry, says Skip Rapp, founder and owner.

Do I detect an implication here that women were not serious skiers in 1984?

"The perception most manufacturers and retailers had is that women preferred to do their skiing in the lodge," Rapp says. "But now they are more receptive to the rising voice of young professional women demanding equality in all areas of their lives."

Women speak. Hard Corps listens.

In the 1993/94 ski season, Hard Corps introduced its first women's technical line made like the men's. It includes weather-protective features and fabrics like sturdy hoods, high collars, lots of Gore-Tex, ballistic nylon shoulder protection for carrying skis (it's less bulky in the women's suits), and pockets for avalanche beepers.

"They are not de-tuned garments for women," Rapp says. "The big-shoulder, narrow-waist look is for freedom of movement for the attractive athlete. Our clothes have become a political statement for female skiers."

An interesting note: Hard Corps' research shows that skiers indicate strong interest in technical ski clothes in the West, the Rocky Mountain region and New England. The research shows some interest in the Midwest and not much in the South or Southern California.

"The percentage of hard-core female skiers out there you could put in your ear," argues Linda Klein, the outspoken co-owner of Willi's Ski Shop in Pittsburgh, Pennsylvania.

Klein began a career in ski retailing nearly 30 years ago, "since the days of lace-up boots," as she puts it. The family-owned store, nationally recognized for its excellence, was named "Eastern Retailer of the Year" for 1994 by Ski Industries America.

"The extreme-ski look is not up my alley," Klein says, "and the majority of women are like me."

When women ask for technical lines, Klein believes they're asking for durable fabric and construction that will keep them warm and dry, but also looking good. Women in the National Skier Opinion Survey rank warmth, style and color on top of the list of considerations when buying ski apparel.

But what technical means to skiwear designers is the mountaineering look or the uniform look of the ski team, instructors and ski patrol, Klein says.

"We wanted technical fabrics; we got men's suits in women's sizes," she laments. "Women don't need pit zips; the last thing we worry about is sweating. I counted 11 zippers on one jacket. We don't want armor; we want style!"

Klein applauds **North Face** for its designs that include a softer technical look for its women's line. Other technical lines entering the women's market include **Gerry,** whose value-priced jackets cost no more than $200, **Degre 7, Marker Ltd., Marmot**, and **Spyder**.

If you're into making a style statement on the slopes, rather than a political one, there are plenty of companies to fulfill your high-fashion fancy, including **Nils** and its signature empire-waisted stretch suit, elegant **Skea, Silvy Tricot** and fur-trimmed **M. Miller**. There's also **Bogner,** whose classic skiwear designs have become status symbols, and **Sport Obermeyer,** whose clothing for women has wide appeal. Klein says Obermeyer's success is a result of listening to consumers. Its clothes are consistently comfortable, warm, good-looking and affordable.

Whichever look you're after, you can't go wrong if you stick with major skiwear brands made with weatherproof fabrics and well-planned features.

Just for women

The line that best combines fashion with practicality is **Lundstrom,** the work of the innovative Canadian designer Linda Lundstrom. Designed for women skiers by a woman skier, her collection is feminine and romantic in feeling but engineered with the latest technologies for warmth. More than any other designer, her clothing addresses special needs of women, such as drop-seat pants, a multi-convertible jacket with a built-in "back-packer" for hanging the jacket on your back, a safety whistle on the front zipper, and reflective tape on pockets and back. Her mix-and-match ski components coordinate with apres-ski sportswear, footwear and accessories. Jackets range from $400 to $600; "washroom" pants are about $300; one-piece powder suits start at about $680.

For a bit of *femme fatale* fun on the slopes, **Vi-Ski** makes the Ultimate Lady ski *skirt*. The ankle-length, flared skirt connects to empire-waisted two-way stretch wool leggings, making it a unique one-piece skirt-pant outfit with matching jacket of insulated, weather-proof nylon. If you think the long skirt might get in your way, there's a smashing mini-ski-skirt, certainly a conversation piece in the lift line. The jacket retails for around $275; the long skirt-pant about $450; the mini about $350.

Large or tall women who don't ski, or quit because they couldn't find warm clothing, need look no further. **Beautiful S-K-I-E-R** specializes in oversized skiwear for women. The company carries a complete line of stylish, high-quality clothing, underwear and accessories. Sizes run from 16 to 30 in jackets and pants, which come with a 30-inch inseam. Tall sizes range from 6 to 20 in jackets; 6 to 18 in pants with a 36-inch inseam. Prices are reasonable.

Warmth is not just for wimps

Whatever your preference — high fashion or high tech — warmth is always in. My survey shows that being cold puts a freeze on a woman's ability to enjoy skiing, and it's one of the reasons women quit skiing.

When buying ski clothes, the first consideration should be your body chemistry: Are you warm-blooded or cold-blooded? Combined with where you usually ski and the amount of energy you put out, knowing this can help you decide how much warmth you need.

Layering continues to be the smartest way to foil foul weather. Warm air trapped between layers of clothing creates insulation that keeps you warmer than a single piece of heavier clothing.

Underwear

The clothing layer closest to your body should be made of a fiber that wicks perspiration, keeping your skin warm and dry. Look for long underwear with moisture-moving fibers and fabrics such as **Thermax, Transpor, Thermastat, Capilene** and **Dryline.** Cotton and cotton blends absorb and retain water, leaving your skin cold and damp. Silk feels warm, soft and luxurious next to your skin, but when it's wet, doesn't work as well as other fibers. Look for good ski underwear at ski and outdoor-sports shops, not department stores.

In your t-shirt and unisex long johns, do you ever feel like a lumberjack? Give them to your husband (he's OK).

Now, you can wear **Wintimates,** feminine, fashionable and functional thermal bodywear from Jackson Jill, a company based in Jackson, Wyoming. Jill is lingerie designer Jill Woodard.

Wintimates' sleek, sexy, shapely bodysuits are constructed for a woman's curves and fit like a second skin. They're available in two styles: snap-crotch bodysuits (about $70) with matching leggings (about $40), and full-length, one-piece union suits featuring drop seats or fanny flaps (suggested retail: $98-$113).

Wintimates are made of *Thermastat* and *Lycra Spandex* for a four-way stretch. Some feature built-in bust support; others are accented with lace; all are fitted and flattering. Think about it: one less shirttail bunching up under your ski pants!

Middle layer

On top of thermalwear, the next layer should be a turtleneck (polyester is better than cotton) topped by a fleece pullover or jacket. With its new weather-resistant treatments, fleece holds as much warmth as a traditional ski sweater, plus it resists moisture and wicks away perspiration.

If you choose a sweater, make it wool or wool-blend. Wool wicks moisture from the skin and retains heat well; sweatshirts absorb perspiration and stay damp, losing body heat.

Outer layer

The final layer should be the insulated or non-insulated parka and pant, or one-piece ski suit. Insulated clothing traps air, creating a barrier that keeps warmth in and cold out. It stays warmer than non-insulated clothing, but for some people can be too warm.

Sport Obermeyer's Barbara Owen explains: "Insulation requirements for an outerwear garment that will be worn with other layers will vary depending on the user's needs. For example, someone skiing on n a damp, cold day will require more insulation than a person skiing where conditions are warmer and drier.

"In general, lightweight insulations are more versatile because they are less bulky and easy to layer over or under. This translates into a greater level of comfort and freedom of movement."

One-piece suits

Once you wear a one-piece suit, you'll never want to go back to pants and parkas. One-piece outfits are comfortable, convenient, figure-flattering and, I think, warmer. It's just your body and lots of trapped warm air in there!

Of the three types — insulated, non-insulated and stretch pants attached to an insulated top — you'll find insulated the warmest.

I love my one-piece ski suits, especially now that I've found a solution to going to the bathroom! Linda Klein laughs with me about it: You get in the stall, take off your goggles and dripping-wet hat and gloves and find there's no place to put them except between your knees.

You unzip and drop your top, trying like hell to keep the sleeves from dragging on the dirty, wet floor. Still clutching your hat, goggles and gloves with your knees (the one time your Q angle proves beneficial!), you fiddle with pulling your long underwear bottoms down around your bum. Then you remember what your mother told you: don't ever sit on the seat!

The price of expensive resorts is justified in my mind by bathroom stalls with racks or wire baskets for loose stuff. And I've solved the problem of dragging one-piece suit sleeves by sewing small clips on the insides of the sleeve cuffs and hooking them to my belt loop when I sit. This way, the sleeves fold up close to my hips and out of reach of the floor. Velcro would work also, one strip inside the suit, the other inside the cuff.

Stretch pants

The two- and four-way stretch materials made of wool, lycra, cotton and nylon blends make fabulous unitards and pants. But they're not as warm as warm-air layered insulated pants or one-piece suits.

In-the-boot pants invite snow and wind to creep into your boot tops. Skiing powder? Out of the question. Also, stretch pants interfere with leg contact with your ski boots (your bootfitter will have a fit!), and the stirrups can cut off circulation in your feet.

Roffe always has made over-the-boot stretch pants, now called "on-the-boot." Unlike the bell-bottoms of the 70s, cuffs zip tight over the boots. You still must deal with a pant liner taking up boot space, however.

If you want to be and look like a serious skier, X the stretch.

Little things mean a lot

Real-estate agents say the key is location, location, location. In ski duds it's details, details, details. You don't realize their importance until you need them.

One beautiful spring morning in Vail, I boarded Chair 3 en route to a St. Patrick's Day picnic. Half-way up, a fierce wind kicked in, swirling snowflakes around us like feathers shaken from a pillow. Wouldn't you know, the lift stopped! There we sat, dangling like wind chimes in this surprise spring storm (Colorado is famous for them.) Naturally, I wasn't wearing a hat. Then, I remembered the hood tucked in the back of my Obermeyer ski suit. I pulled it around my head and was snug as a pea in a pod waiting it out.

Barbara Alley, fashion editor for *Snow Country* magazine, emphasizes that skiers shouldn't be fooled by skiwear in discount or department stores. Though a parka might resemble a brand carried in specialty ski shops, she cautions, its cheaper price tells you the fabric, construction and features are not the same quality and won't protect you from the elements like the real thing.

Features to look for:

- Wind flaps over zippers for wind and snow protection.
- Pull-tabs on zippers for easy grabbing with mittens or gloves
- Strategically-placed pockets for outside access, such as a trail map pocket on a pantleg.
- No hip pockets on tight-fitting pants — they make for too much bulk.
- Sealed seams — wind can rip through seams of poorly made clothes.
- Snug or adjustable cuffs at wrists and ankles.
- Collars and inside closures that can be zipped or buckled up to the chin.
- Elasticized drawstrings at waists and hems of jackets that can be tightened for protection from the elements.

Buying tips

• Bring long underwear, turtleneck and sweater to ensure a good fit for trying on ski clothes.

• Sit and squat in pants or suits to make sure they don't ride up. For all-day, active wear, they must be roomy.

• If leg length looks too long, it's probably OK. Remember, ski boots add about an inch.

• Too loose appears more flattering than too tight.

• Black and dark navy create a more slimming silhouette than any other color, particularly in pants.

• A jacket with a long peplum looks better on big hips than a short one. This belted style emphasizes big shoulders, narrow waist and legs.

• Don't be afraid of white. Water-repellent coatings also contain stain repellent tough enough to be scrubbed. Most fabrics can be machine washed, but always follow instructions. (DuPont makes a waterstain-repeller laundry additive under its **Second Wind** label.)

• One-piece suits cost less than two-piece outfits, but you can wear a long jacket over leggings or slacks, doubling its use.

Accessories

Matching accessories can make a nice outfit really great. Alley suggests buying two T-necks or sweaters for the same outfit for a change in color. Many manufacturers make color-coordinated hats, headbands, neck warmers and sweaters.

It's a good idea to buy them at the time you make your major purchase because other stores may not carry that brand. Three years ago, I bought a gorgeous mauve Head suit and I'm still trying to find a hat!

Hats and headbands

Headwear sections of ski shops are looking more and more like costume departments. With the snowboarders' influence, hats express more freedom and fun. If dredlocks, cone heads, the Scrunch, the Octopus, Jughead, Robin Hood or the Annie Hall style aren't your type, there remain plenty of traditional styles.

Several brands make hats, headbands or ear muffs featuring pockets over the ears for inserting disposable heat packs.

Alley says she likes the look of a long neck warmer pulled up over the head and crossed with a matching headband. She reminds us that half our body heat escapes through our head. Keeping your vital organs warm and covering your head will help hold heat in fingers and toes.

When my children were little and trying to be responsible for their ski gear, I taught them to think in threes: hat, goggles and gloves; skis, boots and poles. To this day, I use this rule — except I've added neck gator to the list. When my neck is bundled in fleece up to my nose, my whole body stays warm!

Gloves and mittens

Keeping hands dry ranks as important as keeping them warm, because hands lose heat 30 times faster when they're wet. Look for gloves or mittens made with high-tech insulations and materials for heat retention and water resistance. Mittens stay warmer than gloves and mittens with liners are warmer yet.

Many gloves and mittens feature pockets for inserting heat packs for those bitter cold days. Expect to spend from $40 to $100 for good hand protection.

On disposable heat packs:

• **Heat Factory** makes them for hands and feet, but don't substitute one for the other — they can burn your palms. If you've held on to unopened packs from last year, you can use them this season; they're good for two to three years. A single pack costs $1; a pair about $2.50. Small-size packs for kids are available, too.

• The Heat Flow glove, featuring a heated-liquid system, works like this: Insert an activated heat pack in the glove's wrist pocket, which adjoins a liner containing a non-toxic fluid. Normal hand movements circulate the heated fluid in the liner, warming the entire hand. On less cold days, omit the heat pack and the liner will capture natural body heat and distribute it. **Zero** makes the gloves and mittens, both of which retail for about $26. **Swany** and **Grandoe** make similar products.

Thin glove liners made with moisture-moving materials work well inside gloves or mittens for added warmth and dryness. I like mine when I need to use my fingers outside my gloves for taking notes or opening trail maps.

Cold feet

If cold feet are a chronic problem, or if you can't feel your toes while skiing, your boots could be cutting off circulation. Next time you take them off, check your feet and lower legs immediately. If you see any bulging blood vessels, this means they're pumping blood to get it back to the toes. It's an indication your boots are too tight in that spot. A bootfitter can correct this.

Nothing makes you more miserable than wet, clammy feet. Pedorthist Jeff Rich says the average skier's foot sheds half a pint of perspiration a day on the slopes. Wearing the right kind of ski socks and taking a few simple precautions can prevent perspiration and circulation problems that cause cold feet.

Warm socks

• Socks should be made of the same moisture-wicking materials that is used for long underwear is made. **ProperSox** uses a material called Transpor, a new fiber that transfers vapor and perspiration from the skin without soaking the sock. One way to determine a fiber's resistance to saturation is by observing how fast it dries. When I take my socks from the washer, they're hardly wet and line dry in a flash. Cotton socks, on the other hand, take forever in a dryer. **Thorlo** and **Wigwam** brands also are good ski socks.

• Layering does not apply to socks. Wear one thin sock (about the weight of a men's dress sock). Heavier socks or layering will create more perspiration and circulation problems.

• Pantyhose and nylon workout tights do *not* make good substitutes for ski socks. They contribute to cold feet in women more than anything. The reason: Nylon doesn't allow feet to breathe, making them wet and clammy. Nylon also makes feet slide in the boots, causing loss of steering and edging control.

• Wear clean socks every day. Dirt and perspiration interfere with wicking, causing loss of thermal quality.

• Wipe your feet dry before putting on socks and never put on boots when socks still are damp.

• Don't put on wet or cold boots. Your feet will stay wet and cold all day, making them susceptible to blisters and frostbite. When you drive to a ski area, keep your boots on the heated floor of the front seat.

• Take the liners out of the shells at night to dry out. This also will help prolong their life. If you have trouble removing or putting liners back in, **Air Dry Systems** makes a nifty portable dryer, The Evaporator, that dries two pairs of boots overnight with cool, circulating air. (Don't dry boots with a hair dryer. The hot air can melt insoles and break down materials.) The Evaporator, excellent for traveling, retails for about $89.

Boot heaters

More and more women are discovering boot heaters as a great way to keep their tootsies toasty. The heating system consists of a small, rechargeable battery pack that attaches to the back of your boots by screws or a removable strap. It plugs into wires that flow to a heating element on the footbed, which warms your foot.

- **Hotronics** is favored by ski instructors in the Northeast, where cold can be brutal. It has four heat settings for durations of 55 minutes to eight hours. Suggested retail price: $149.

- **Winter Heat** lasts from one to three hours and is the smallest unit. Price: about $130.

- **Extreme Comfort** costs the least (about $80) and runs from one-and-a-half to six hours.

- **Sure Heat's** heating element envelops the bottom and top of the toes and uses two-and-a-half times the battery power of other brands; about $100.

If you use any of these heaters, make sure the battery pack is secure. Packs that clip on the back of boots can be knocked off when you're riding the chair lift or going down stairs.

Because of the popularity of boot heaters, Seirus stopped making the neoprene Boot Masque, which fit like spats over ski boots. But Seirus' company rep Joe Edwards says the product is likely to be resurrected as a less expensive alternative (about $40 a pair) to boot heaters.

NOTE: Before spending big bucks on a sport you're trying out, borrow ski clothes from your skiing friends. Or you can rent skiwear at a ski rental shop. You may not create a fashion sensation, but at least you'll be warm. Don't wear blue jeans — they soak up snow and stay wet all day.

Chapter Summary:
This chapter serves as a handy reference guide for fibers, fabrics and fillings of winter wear. You learned tips that, hopefully, will keep you warm, dry and comfortable from head to toe.

Product information:

Ski clothing brands mentioned in this chapter can be found in most U.S. retail ski shops. The following can be ordered by mail:

Lundstrom — U.S. sales representative: Leslie Trudeau, Trudeau & Co., P.O. Box 701, Oconomowoc, WI, 53066; (312) 467-9118; (800) 66LINDA; (800) 665-4632..

Ultimate Lady Ski Skirt — Vi-Ski, Vickie Hodges, 16803 McLean Road, Pearland, TX 77584; (713) 489-0055; FAX (713) 489-3655.

Beautiful S-K-I-E-R — distributed by Seven Brothers International Inc., 41 Wilson Lane, New Boston, NH 03070; (603) 487-3334; (800) 638-3334.

Wintimates — Jackson Jill, P.O. Box 8849, Jackson, WY 83001; (307) 739-0866.

If you can't find these products in ski shops, call to learn where you can find them in your area.

Air Dry Systems (800) 237-6779.
Extreme Comfort — (800) 845-6098.
Grandoe (800) 472-6363.
Heat Factory (714) 472-8928.
Hotronics (802) 862-7403.
ProperSox (612) 930-0500.
Sure Heat — (800) 887-HEAT; (800) 877-4328.
Swany (800) 237-9269.
Thorlo (800) 438-0209.
Wigwam (800) 558-7760.
Winter Heat (800) 222-5880.
Zero (800) 247-3383.

Chapter Eleven

Mountain Mamas

"When I am skiing I gain strength, energy, spirit and a true sense of being alive in a vibrant way."
— *Dianne, age 45 from California*

Y ou don't have to be an expert to appreciate the aesthetics of skiing. The winter outdoors, the natural beauty of the mountains, glorious views, fresh air, and closeness to nature are the most frequent answers to my survey question, "What do you love about skiing?" Others mentioned the sound of skis on the snow, the warm sun and the solitude. Marcela from Mexico likes just "seeing the snow!"

Exercise and the challenge of skiing are listed second. Again, all ability groups agree on this. Vicki, 37, from Colorado, sums it up: "I like doing something hard and good with my body!"

Exhilaration, feeling free and the rush of flying down the mountain rank a close third. Many women say they're happy with the feeling of well-being after a day on the slopes and the satisfaction of "getting it."

Twenty-eight-year-old Sue from Massachusetts says she likes "Feeling good about myself when I perform well." Catherine, 24 from Wyoming, skis 70 days a year and "loves the floating, airy feeling I get when I make good turns." Melissa, 29, an instructor at Telluride, is completely in tune with her sport: She loves "the glide, the cuts through gravity, the feeling of controlled falling, the power of the ski."

There is nothing like being on top of the world under a blue canopy of sky. People who don't ski never get the opportunity to experience the mountains as we do.

Rare mountain air

But the best of days can be marred by high-altitude sickness or acute mountain sickness. Anyone who ascends from sea level or the lowlands to the thin atmosphere of higher altitudes can be affected. In Colorado, where the average resort's base elevation measures 8,764 feet above sea level, the air contains 40 percent *less oxygen* and 50 percent *less humidity* than air at sea level.

A sudden change in environment can bring on headache, sleeplessness, fatigue, shortness of breath, nausea and vomiting. These conditions can come on from six hours to two days after you arrive and persist for as long as a week, although a few days is more common. If symptoms do persist and become severe, see a doctor immediately. Acute mountain sickness is not something you can condition yourself for, and you won't know if you're susceptible until it happens.

Take simple precautions

• Give yourself one or two days to acclimate. Avoid heavy exercise — don't jump off the plane and onto the slopes. Plan your vacation accordingly.

• Push the fluids to prevent dehydration. You should drink at least eight 12-oz. glasses of water daily. This is easy — you're thirsty anyway from the loss of moisture due to low humidity.

• Alcohol is not one of the fluids you should push, at least not the first two or three days, and you should lighten up on it the rest of the time. Alcohol contributes to dehydration and affects breathing. Substitute water or fruit juice for your second après-ski drink.

• Cut back on caffeine, which is also dehydrating. Adding a little milk or cream to coffee will dilute caffeine.

• Eat lightly. Go for high-carbohydrate foods like whole-grain breads, cereals, pasta, rice, fruits and vegetables. You'll feel better if you eat several small meals a day instead of three large ones.

When Didi Lawrence taught skiing at Beaver Creek, she introduced me to a lunch of a baked potato with cottage cheese and a dollop of low-fat honey-mustard dressing, sprinkled with black olives and pepper. Yum! Many ski areas feature salad bars with baked potatoes and offer grilled chicken breasts and healthful pizzas.

In areas of low humidity, increased activity can cause nosebleeds. Be prepared with a jar of Vaseline for a few dabs in the nose every morning and night. This, plus plenty of fluids, should cure the problem.

Skin care

We all know we're exposed to even more dangerous levels of ultraviolet radiation now with the depletion of the ozone layer. Skiers risk even more damage from the sun at mountain elevations. Reflections off the snow intensify the sun's effect as well.

With most skiers hitting the slopes from around 10 a.m. to 3 p.m., precisely the hours when the sun's rays are strongest, we need to be vigilant about protecting our skin.

Barbara Reed, a Colorado dermatologist, warns that ultraviolet rays increase 2 percent with every 1,000 feet of elevation above sea level. In the Colorado mountains, for example, where skiers ride lifts to around 12,000 feet, they're exposed to 24 percent more ultraviolet rays than on a Hawaiian beach!

Because 80 percent of ultraviolet rays are *reflected* off of snow, a sun visor or a hat with a brim doesn't help much. The best defense is sunscreen slathered on face, lips, and especially nose and ears, which are more susceptible to malignancies. You can also make like a bandit when it's sunny *and* cold by wearing a ski mask. Don't be fooled by gray days: 80 percent of ultraviolet rays penetrate clouds.

• *UVA and UVB*

Remember that sun affects skin two ways: The burning ray, UVB, causes skin cancer; the aging ray, UVA, causes skin damage. UVA, which can pass through glass and penetrate deeper into the skin, usually doesn't burn; however, it causes wrinkles, liver spots and sagging tissue.

• *Sunscreens*

While all sunscreens protect from UVB rays, Dr. Reed says only one brand offers *more extensive* protection against UVA. **Shade UVA Guard** contains Parsol 1789, an ingredient found to battle the full spectrum of UVA rays. Other brands contain a less inclusive UVA shield. Shade UVA Guard is sold over the counter in drug, grocery and discount stores.

If your skin is sensitive or allergic, products made for children are less harsh, won't sting your eyes and contain no PABA, which causes allergic reactions in many people. (PABA also can permanently stain clothing.)

If you have fair skin or have undergone a facelift, chemical peel or dermabrasion, or if you regularly use Retin-A, cortisone creams, or alpha hydroxy acids on your face, you must be extra careful. Your skin is thinner and more sun-sensitive. Ditto for expectant mothers and women taking birth control pills or hormones. Hormonal states can cause a discoloration on the face and neck that the sun can intensify. Use sunscreen liberally if any of these exceptions apply to you.

Don't wait until you get to the mountains to pull out your sunscreen and lip balm. Dr. Reed suggests wearing sunscreen during the drive up. "We see more skin cancers and pre-cancers on the left side of the face (of skiers who drive west)," Reed says. Sun can be intense, beating through a car window.

The time to smear on sunscreen is 30 minutes before going into the sun. Throughout your ski day, reapply every 90 minutes if the sun is bright, if perspiration causes you to wipe your face, or if a runny nose has you wiping it often. Areas that have sunburned before are delicate and require heavier sun block. Says Dr. Reed: "This is really, really important."

- ## *SPF rating*

When sunscreen testers try out a product, they heavily apply the cream, then give it an SPF number, a multiple of the number of minutes you can remain in the sun without burning. If you usually burn in 15 minutes without sunblock, a sunblock of SPF 2 would allow you to be in the sun 30 minutes without burning.

Dr. Reed reminds us the ratings are derived from heavily applied sunscreen in test laboratories — not the lighter coating most people use — and usually pertain to sun at sea-level intensity. Experts recommend an SPF of at least 15 for most people. At higher altitudes, use products with a rating even higher than 15.

Hats, especially baseball caps, will not make you sun safe. If you can see the sun through your hat, burning rays can get through. Hair sprays with sunscreen, such as Topcoat by **Dermatone**, are recommended for people with thin hair who want to ski hatless or with a head band. Give the part in your hair a shot, too. Choose a pump spray — it penetrates more directly than an aerosol. This product also works great in preventing scalp-burn on the balding men in your life.

- ## *Frostbite*

Sunburn's effects are more long-term than frostbite's, but frostbite can be dangerous if untreated. Caused by extreme cold when blood vessels constrict so that blood cells cannot pass through them, frostbite turns affected skin unnaturally white and numb. Most susceptible to frostbite: ears, noses, hands and feet.

Treatment should be immediate. Cover the affected skin and ski to a shelter or mountain lodge. Restore circulation gradually, warming the affected skin under blankets, clothing, or warm — not hot! — water. Never rub frostbitten skin because you could further damage tissue. Once flesh is frostbitten, it may remain especially sensitive to cold. Special care should be taken to keep affected areas warm and dry.

Some skin-protector products guard against frostbite by allowing you to stay in the cold longer, as well as lessening the severity of damage. Ask about them at your drugstore's pharmacy.

Though she's never treated a case like this, Dr. Reed says it's conceivable that the telltale whitening of a frostbitten spot on the face could go unnoticed under heavy makeup. So, save your model look for night life. Sunscreen and the natural, healthy glow from crisp, clean air are the only makeup you need on the slopes. Frequent applications of SPF 15 lip gloss will keep your lips shiny and the cold will give your cheeks a rosy hue.

• *Frost nip*

Some women are affected by Raynaud's Disease, a disorder of the small blood vessels of the hands and feet. In cold weather — not necessarily just severe cold — vessels constrict, blocking blood flow and turning the skin white, then blue. If you suffer from chronically cold hands and feet, take extra care to keep them warm. Immediately treat cold hands by vigorously moving your arms in big circles to get blood circulating to the fingers.

• **Hot tubs**

There is nothing like a moonlight soak in a hot tub after a day of cold skiing. It feels soooo good! But if your skin is sensitive, the extreme heat and harsh chemicals can cause a prickly rash and burning sensation. If you can't resist the hot tub, take a *brief* dip, then follow immediately with a shower to wash off the chemicals. Then, smooth non-perfumed lotion liberally over your entire body. (Perfumes can irritate sensitive skin or cause an allergic reaction.)

Eye care

Meticulous care should be taken to protect your eyes from sun when you're skiing. Ophthalmologist Joel Goldstein says he has treated hundreds of cases of sunburned eyes in his practices in Denver and Vail.

"People get fooled when it's overcast or cloudy, and ski without eye protection," Goldstein explains. "After skiing, they feel OK. Their eyes may be a little red but they go to dinner and out partying. Then, about 3 or 4 in the morning, they wake up in pain." Eye sunburn requires immediate medical attention.

• **eyeware**

Goggles, wrap-around shields, or sunglasses with side covers protect eyes and the delicate skin around them from damaging sun.

Eyewear should be considered as part of your basic ski equipment, not as accessories. Women skiers often shun goggles for more flattering sunglasses, but when light turns flat or weather becomes stormy, dark-lens sunglasses are worthless as eye protection.

A good pair of yellow-lens goggles acts like a glass house for your eyes: It protects them from the elements and vastly improves vision by increasing contrasts in snow. Don't go skiing without them.

Goggles cost from $20-$200. Useless if they fog up, make sure they're anti-fog — usually these are made with double lenses. Applied frequently, defogging solutions and cloths will work. Never wipe goggles with tissue or paper toweling because their abrasive surfaces will damage anti-fog coatings. Either use a soft cloth or let your goggles air dry.

Try on goggles before you buy them. I've found several pairs with wavy lenses that distorted my vision. Women's models, designed for smaller faces, might fit better than unisex styles. Too-big goggles also look geeky and allow cold air to leak through the gaps.

Goggles that fit over eyeglasses are available — ask for OTG models. **Bolle** makes a nifty adapter frame for people who wear prescription eyewear: an optical shop inserts prescription lenses into a frame that snaps into certain models of Bolle glasses and goggles. **Carrera** makes goggles for contact lenses (OTC) with special air venting.

Shields are an alternative to goggles. They fit over the ears like sunglasses but wrap around the face, providing protection similar to goggles.

Sunglasses are categorized in three types by the U.S. Food and Drug Administration: cosmetic, general-purpose and special-purpose. The optical clarity and color treatment best for high altitude glare is in special-purpose lenses. You'll find them in ski shops, optical stores and some opticians' offices, but not at grocery, drug, or discount department stores. Prices begin at $30 for plastic lenses and can go up to $250 for quality glass lenses. Don't buy lenses offering anything less than 100-percent protection from ultraviolet rays. If you're wondering about ultraviolet protection, most optical shops will read the UV level of your sunglasses at no charge.

For maximum protection, wear lenses with gray or green lenses or a combination of these colors for bright sun. You'll do better with yellow lenses on overcast days. Leave the mirrored lenses to the movie stars: they scratch and act like a magnet for UV rays to your face.

Protect your eyewear: Store frames and goggles in hard-cover cases. (Glass case, under $10; goggles case, about $8. To order, call (916) 926-2600; FAX (800) 926-9904.) During your lunch break, don't toss goggles in the pile of gloves and hats that builds up on the table. I've seen expensive goggles ruined from food spills. Instead, wear them backward around your neck, on top of your head, or around your arm — you'll protect them from scratching and breaking this way, too.

Skiers from areas of high humidity and low altitude find their eyes dry out at high altitude resorts with low humidity. Because *dry eyes are more susceptible to burning*, Dr. Goldstein recommends carrying a tube of over-the-counter artificial tears while you ski. Apply five or six times a day. (The non-preserved solution is less likely to cause an allergic reaction than preserved.) People who wear contact lenses find dry eyes a nuisance and should follow this advice.

Hair care

Hat hair, matte hair ... every ski day is a bad-hair day for women! Not all of us have long, thick tresses we can pull away from our faces and weave into luxurious braids. But your hair can stay healthy and shiny even after long hours of fun in the sun.

"The best thing you can do for your hair when skiing is to cover it," says Denver hairdresser Mary Ann McGreggor. As with skin, sun reflecting off snow and beating down overhead can damage hair, especially if it's chemically treated.

McGreggor's high-altitude hair-care prescription:

• Shampoo in the shower.

• Use an inexpensive, generic baby shampoo that is *not* pH-balanced. If the product lathers well the first time, don't shampoo again. Rinse completely.

• Apply a moisturizer — not a conditioner — according to directions. (Vidal Sassoon's Protein Remoisturizer is great.) Moisturizers penetrate the hair and keep it flexible; conditioners coat it, leaving it dull and lifeless. Unless you're in the sun a lot, you don't need to moisturize all of your hair with every shampoo; just work in a little on the ends, which tend to get dry and brittle.

• While rinsing out moisturizer, run a wide-toothed comb through your hair with the rinse water. Don't pull too hard. Let the water and the moisturizer untangle your hair.

• Pour an acidic rinse over your head made with one part vinegar or lemon juice diluted with 20 parts water. This step is essential.

• Rinse lightly with warm water.

• Blot, do not rub, your hair with a towel. With long hair, wrap the ends in a towel and ring moisture out.

As for hat hair, First Lady of Ski Fashion Barbara Alley wears a *balaclava*, a silk hood for the head and neck, under her knit hat. Her red mane doesn't get as mashed as when she wears the hat directly on her hair. (Balaclavas are found in catalogs that sell silk underwear.)

For a quick touchup for après-ski, try a curling iron that runs on propane. It can be used anywhere and is light enough to carry in a backpack or fanny pack. A travel-size hair spray can be packed with it. You'll find the curling iron wherever hair appliances are sold.

NOTE: If you don't find sunscreen or hair-care products in health and beauty sections of drug and grocery stores, ask your pharmacist. Or look in catalogs of network sales marketing companies such as Avon or Amway.

Skiing for two

To ski pregnant is a choice mothers-to-be should make with their physician based on level of fitness as well as comfort threshold. If you're not relaxed, you may fall more easily. Although the fetus is fairly well protected in the amniotic fluid, any injury suffered by a woman during pregnancy can be more complicated because doctors are more hesitant to prescribe medication.

My obstetrician and gynecologist, Donald Bennallack, says that the hormone relaxin causes ligaments to loosen during pregnancy, making them more prone to tearing in a fall.

"I tell my patients to just take it easy," Bennallack advises.

I skied through five healthy pregnancies and found that my protective instincts took over, making it easy for me to proceed slowly and in control. I shunned difficult slopes and skied on the sides of crowded runs. I rested a lot. During my daughter's pregnancy, her doctor advised her not to let her heart rate go higher than 140 beats a minute and to avoid extremes in temperature.

Clothes are definitely a problem, but pregnant skiers learn to improvise. Most don't ski when their tummies are really large. One garment everyone agrees on is a good support bra!

Telluride ski instructor Cindy Smith, who skied during two pregnancies, found that her stance and balance improved. She felt more grounded and moved more effectively with her skis. "Skiing during pregnancy," she says, "is a great way to feel light again — letting gravity do most of the work."

You might notice that your boots fit differently after you've given birth because most women's feet grow wider during pregnancy. Your bootfitter can make necessary adjustments. Also, the DIN setting of your bindings may need to be reset if you haven't gotten back to your pre-baby weight.

The mid-life skier

There is no better time for skiing than in mid-life. The children are raised, there usually is more disposable time and income, lift-ticket prices are lower for seniors, and at most resorts, after 70, skiing is *free!*

Skiers 50 and older can even belong to their own ski club: **Over the Hill Gang, International.** More than 3,200 members in 50 states and 13 countries enjoy skiing and schmoozing with other outdoor enthusiasts "in the prime of life."

Membership includes: Discounts on lift tickets, meals, lodging, transportation, and equipment rentals (detailed in a benefit directory); frequent ski and summer adventure trips in this country and abroad; a learn-to-ski program tailored to older skiers.

You can join this international club through chapter membership ($62 for a single; $100 a couple). Local groups host social events and ski trips of their own. If there's no Gang in your area, you can join as an at-large member for $37 or $60. For information, write to 3310 Cedar Heights Drive, Colorado Springs, CO 80904; or call (719) 685-4656; FAX (719) 685-4162.

The "changing" woman skier

A few health concerns for menopausal women:

• Because of the overall "drying out" in this hormonal state, some women will experience more eye dryness.

• Loss of muscle mass can be detrimental, but if older women maintain a regular routine of strength training, they can build muscle power to match that of younger women.

• The greatest health concerns for post-menopausal skiers are fractures to bones weakened by osteoporosis, a disease that thins bone tissue. Women experience significant bone loss during the five to seven years after menopause when their bodies stop producing estrogen.

For women in menopause, most physicians recommend hormone-replacement therapy, 1,000 mg. of calcium daily (or 1,500 for those not taking hormones), weight-bearing exercise, and a healthy lifestyle. Skiing fills half of this prescription perfectly!

Younger women and teens can reduce their risk of osteoporosis by eating calcium-rich foods like dairy products, leafy green vegetables, sardines and salmon. Calcium supplements can boost daily intake to 1,200-1,500 mg. recommended by the National Institute of Health for ages 11 to 24, the peak years for building bone density. Women 25 to 50 should take in 1,000 mg.

Risk factors increasing a woman's chances for osteoporosis include heredity, fair skin, light frame, childlessness, diabetes mellitus, excessive alcohol consumption, smoking, high protein and phosphorus intake and lack of exercise. Unfortunately, bone density tests for diagnosing osteoporosis detect it only after irreversible damage already has occurred.

Smoking and skiing

We all know smoking and exercise don't mix. A 1994 study indicates that tears to the rotator cuff, a group of muscles surrounding the shoulder joint, are more severe in smokers than non-smokers. Rotator-cuff injuries are common among skiers who fall on shoulders or an outstretched arm.

Bare necessities

If you're flying to a resort, carry on a bag containing items you can't live without or don't want to pay high resort prices for in case of lost or delayed luggage. Some of the most important: your ski boots (once you get them to fit right, you don't even want to think about not skiing in them!); medication, knee brace, contact lenses and cleaning solutions or glasses (whichever you're not wearing), and tampons.

Once in Jackson Hole, where three men are available for every woman, a hotel clerk told me she didn't know of a place in Teton Village that sold feminine hygiene products. I finally discovered a convenience store where Tampax was tucked behind the motor oil and chewing tobacco.

Playtex Portables or Tampax Compak are half the size of regular tampons and fit neatly in a ski jacket or fanny pack.

One of my skiing necessities is Advil, which I rely on to relieve swelling and pain from a bulging disc in my lower back. I have always taken my pills on the sly, not wanting to be known as a pill popper. One ski trip changed that. I was on a bus traveling on the Icefields Parkway to Lake Louise in Alberta, Canada. When we approached the ski area, I was wondering where I was going to find water to take my Advil.

All of a sudden I heard Velcro ripping, buckles snapping and zippers zipping. I looked around to find almost everyone strapping on knee braces, back braces and supports of all kinds, and ingesting every brand of ibuprofen on the market. One young photographer from Utah with a bad back carried a veritable medicine chest in his backpack. It was comforting to know I wasn't the only one who needed more than sunscreen to prepare for my day on the mountain!

Chapter Summary:

The best of ski days can be marred for women by high altitude sickness, sunburn, frostbite, Raynaud's Disease, and eye burn. Even hair needs special attention in high, dry climates. In this chapter you learned tips for protection and prevention. We talked about skiing pregnant and skiing in mid-life and reviewed the bare necessities to carry with you on the plane.

Product information:

For brands of sunscreen that contain the best protection against high-altitude sun, send a stamped, self-addressed business-size envelope to: **The Skin Cancer Foundation**, Box 561, Dept. SR, New York, NY 10156.

Dermatone sunscreen, frostbite protection and hair-care products are distributed by **Swix Sport USA**, 261 Ballardvale St., Wilmington, MA 01887; (800) 343-8335.

Bolle America, 3890 Elm St., Denver, CO 80207; (303) 321-4300; FAX (303) 321-6952.

Carrera International Corp., 35 Maple St., Norwood, NJ 07648; (201) 767-3820; FAX (201) 767-8984.

Chapter Twelve

Black diamonds can be a girl's best friend

"I want to ski smoothly — only leg movements and a quiet body — with completed turns and facing down the fall line with no hesitation when there's a terrain change. No upper body swing ... in my dreams!"
— Adele, age 48 from Colorado

Graceful, smooth, fluid. When women in my survey described how they wanted to perform on skis, these are the words they mentioned most often. We all would like to experience these sensations on the slopes more than we do.

Such masterful moments can quickly change to Maalox moments if a soft surface turns icy, or terrain drops like a trap door, or skis sink out of sight in deep powder. *Screech* ... and we revert back to the old reliable sophomore snowplow.

Sound familiar? Then this chapter is for you. Women ski instructors and racers share tips for skiing the hard stuff: ice, bumps, steeps, powder. They also cover running gates and skiing in control.

Skiing in control

Women in my survey said they need to feel in control to ski successfully. One woman, a veteran of 10 years on the slopes, said she still didn't think she had her act together.

"When I feel in control, confident and comfortable on any terrain," she wrote, "I will be completely satisfied. Then people will look at me from the lift and say, 'Wow! That woman can ski!'"

Christie Smith has taught skiing for 14 years, working for the last seven as a supervisor at the Vail/Beaver Creek Ski School. Here, she talks about gaining and maintaining control for safe, successful, confident skiing:

> For me, the allure of downhill skiing is the excitement and the adventure. Skiing incorporates our love of fun and freedom, unlocking inhibitions, and providing exhilaration that permeates the soul. How sweet it is to sweep and glide through the illusive whiteness of that other world!"

These feelings of freedom become nil without the element of control. We've all experienced that moment when our skis take on a life of their own. We get going a little too fast — out of control and out of our comfort zone. Skiing in control ensures a safe experience for all, not to mention a successful run.

Balance

Achieving control begins with balance — a relaxed, centered stance over our skis. Picture yourself standing on a small rug on top of a just-waxed hardwood floor. Someone is about to yank the rug out from under you.

How would you react? Your knees and ankles would bend, your arms and hands would extend forward. Your weight would remain solidly over your feet as you looked ahead. This also is the position for balanced skiing. Balance allows you to react to whatever you encounter. It gives control.

Turn shape

The shape of your turn affects control. A turn has a beginning, a middle and an end. If a turn lacks a definite finish phase, speed increases. A series of incomplete turns can lead to speed acceleration and loss of control.

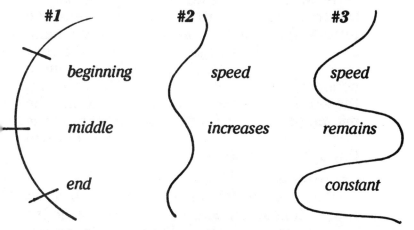

#1 beginning middle end

#2 speed increases

#3 speed remains constant

Practice turn shapes and sizes. To slow each turn, direct your feet across the hill, or think of pointing your skis slightly back up the hill before you begin the next turn. If you want to accelerate, short-cut the finish phase as in diagram two. If you learn to ski a pattern like diagram three, it will be easy to ski the moguls. You can weave through the bumps but remain in control.

Carving the turn

The skill of edging or carving also affects control. Once you master balance and turn shape, you enhance the ski's function by *carving* instead of skidding a turn. A flat ski skidding through a turn will not offer the stability and support of an edged ski.

To feel the difference, traverse the hill on the edges of your skis, keeping your weight on your downhill ski. Then roll your knees and ankles down the slope just enough to release the edges. Feel the skis do a sideslip? Practice making traverses, alternating with sideslips in symmetrical patterns.

Now, take the feeling of edging the ski in a traverse and add it to the finish phase of the turn. Make your turn as you usually would, but tip the ski on edge at the end of the turn (refer to Diagram No. 1). As you become more confident with carving, you can begin to tip the ski on edge earlier in the turn during the middle phase. If you edge your ski during the beginning phase, you will have control throughout the arc.

Awareness

Balance, turn shape and carving make up the technical aspects of control. An active awareness of your skiing environment completes the equation of control equaling safety. Always look ahead. This gives your body time to react naturally to the ever-changing slopes. Be aware of skiers around you. Try to ski a predictable line rather than veering from one side to the other. Skiing is like driving on the freeway: You need to be aware of the cars ahead, behind and to the side, but you drive directly and confidently in your lane.

By using your new control skills, the mountain becomes a safe playground — a source of discovery and adventure.

Skiing on ice

Alison Clayton is a Professional Ski Instructors of America Eastern Division examiner, a member of its national junior education team, and a staff trainer and teacher at Stratton, VT.

As director of Stratton Women's Ski Holidays, Alison sees women who believe their ski technique is good enough to keep them in a comfort zone ... that is, until they encounter the noise, the glare, and the loss of control that too often come with skiing ice. Her advice:

Icy conditions confront skiers all the time, from a few patches here and there to entire hills of ice as a result of the thaw-freeze weather pattern common in the eastern United States. In other ski areas, soft snow gets scraped away by skier traffic, leaving a surface by afternoon like the tile floor in your bathroom.

Whatever the conditions, confidence in your skiing ability will help make the experience more enjoyable.

For success in skiing on ice, it helps to understand and feel the skiing skills, to develop the ability to blend them to suit the snow conditions at hand. Let's review ski mechanics:

The four skills involved in skiing are balance, edging, steering and pressure management.

• Balance keeps your center of mass over your feet and your skis through the arc of a turn.

• Steering, which includes many kinds of rotations, relates to using the muscles in your legs and hips to turn your feet right and left.

• Edging allows you to roll a flat ski onto its edge in appropriate parts of the turn.

• Pressure management deals with applying and releasing pressure to the skis as necessary.

Balance

Balance, the primary component of good skiing, is not a static position. We don't put on our skis, get balanced and set for the rest of the day. (Wouldn't that make it easy!) Instead, we must constantly adjust our center of mass, using large and small muscle movements to maintain active balance throughout our turns.

Knowing where your center of mass lies helps you move it accurately. Use your hip area as a guide. Wider hips create a center of mass a bit lower than your bellybutton; narrow hips put it right in your bellybutton area. Accurately moving your center of mass greatly improves your ability to balance on skis.

As you move through a turn, both gravity and centrifugal force pull your body (and your skis) to the outside of the turn. The grip of your ski edges allows you to steer and hold a chosen line or turn shape. When you're skiing in icy conditions, the tails of your skis won't grip and they skid out from under you. Your body then rotates and leans into the hill, and you loose control. Panic usually follows, and you may ask yourself why you aren't shopping instead!

Don't panic! There are ways to stay standing on ice. Knowing how will make you more confident in all conditions.

Imagine getting out of your car in an icy parking lot, wearing dress shoes with smooth leather soles. You automatically adjust, making gentle, unhurried, slight movements. You know that any abrupt moves will send you flying. You've learned to keep your joints slightly flexed and your body stacked up in total alignment, ready for the slightest slip.

Think about doing the same on skis. As you traverse the ice, keep your body slightly flexed and stay calm. Your muscles should be as relaxed as possible, releasing any tension that could transmit to your skis. With each joint flexed and your spine relaxed and slightly rounded, you can stay balanced. Once you get the hang of it, it should feel just as comfortable as alignment tricks you've learned for other sports.

When your skis are sliding, and your edge grip is inconsistent, maintain a comfortable stance and concentrate on the feeling of being centered. As you progress through the turn, continue to flex your joints in harmony with each other.

Steering

We tend to forget the ankle joint, but successfully skiing on ice depends on it. Feel contact and some pressure on the fronts of your shins as you bend your ankles and move your kneecaps forward over your toes.

Gently, continue through the arc of the turn, flexing your knees only as much as you need to. Move your hips with your feet to maintain a centered position. By flexing all your joints and moving your hips at the same time, you'll still be in balance at the end of the turn. *Gently* is the key word here.

On ice, skiers often steer their feet too fast, creating a skidded, windshield-wiper turn. Take your time! Look a few turns ahead to anticipate your path. Then, steer your skis as you would steer your car around a curve: turn the wheel gradually and smoothly, allowing the rear tires to follow the front tires along the arc. A jerky, quick turn of the wheel will send you skidding. Steer through the entire turn. A round finish controls speed: the slower you want to go, the rounder your turn needs to be. Be patient when skiing on ice.

Edging

Tiptoe through the turn. Too often, skiers abruptly dig in their edges on ice, trying to get control and slow down. Women skiers who do this along with leaning back and inside will skid sideways, uncontrolled. Instead, roll onto the edges gently, but firmly, as the skis progress through the arc.

Use your big and little toes as cues. The ski on the outside gets rolled onto the big-toe side; the ski on the inside gets rolled onto the little toe. Skis remain parallel as they move smoothly from one set of edges to the other. Any harsh movements cause the edges to break from the ice and produce a skid.

Pressure

There are two ways to pressure your skis: side-to-side or fore-and-aft.

Side-to-side means weighting from one ski to the other. On icy surfaces, it's a good idea to distribute your weight more evenly than you would on softer snow. A guideline might be 80 percent on your outside ski and 20 percent on your inside. This provides a stable platform and sure footing, should your outside ski break free. Be careful to remain in balance. Women skiers too often lean to the inside of the turn with their shoulders when adding pressure to the inside ski.

Fore-and-aft pressure distributes weight from the tips to the tails of your skis. When entering a turn, stand more on the balls of your feet by flexing your ankles forward. This puts pressure on the front of the skis. As the tips engage at the start of the turn, gradually adjust your stance so you stand on your whole foot — feeling pressure in the forefoot, the arch and the heel. This is a neutral and centered stance which is the foundation of balanced skiing.

As you develop these skills, you'll see how they can be combined for varying conditions and terrain. The confidence you gain with experience will help cut down the fear most skiers face skiing on ice. And if you're not so scared, you'll ski with more power and grace.

Skiing bumps

The number-one technique improvement listed by the women in my survey was learning to ski the bumps. "Moguls!" wrote one of the women in the survey. "I look at them and can't decide where to go other than away!"

Thirty-two-year-old Susan from Colorado summed it up: "I want to ski bumps smoothly, gracefully and aggressively," she wrote, "preferably in an expensive Descente ski suit and with an outrageous tan and good hair!"

Barbara Sanders is a supervisor of the ski school at California's Mammoth Mountain and a junior examiner of the PSIA Western Division. She says women can learn to ski bumps by refining their basic skills.

Bumps — friend or foe? Why do these round changes in terrain make our knees shake and our confidence nose-dive? Relax. Chances are you already possess the skills necessary to ski these babies. Now, you need to refine these skills, applying them at the right time and place.

One skill I try to develop with my students is dealing with terrain that drops suddenly, as it does on the backside of each bump. If we don't move forward with the terrain, we get stuck in the back seat. This position will launch us across the bump field out of control — not exactly the way we want to ski the moguls.

To help my students get forward, I ask them to do two things:

- Push their tips down by pushing forward on their boots to keep skis in contact with snow.

• Stand up as they do when the chair lift reaches the knoll, bringing hips over feet, sliding forward down the ramp and turning right or left. Now, picture yourself doing this on the slope.

Where to turn

Students always ask where they should turn in the bumps. I tell them to visualize water flowing down a hill, splashing over the tops of some of the bumps, running into the troughs of others. Skiers can splash over the tops of the moguls, run down the sides, or ski in the gullies. Learning to blend these three techniques will let you ski the bump run smooth and fluid.

• The easiest way to begin the turn is to make a slow pivot on top of the bump, where there is the least snow resistance. Continue the turn as you slide down the backside and complete it with your skis rounding the bottom of the mogul in the gully. This completely rounded ending holds the key to speed control. If needed, a quick hockey-stop motion will check your speed even more just before going into the next turn.

• Another good tactic to integrate in your mogul run is to bank against the sides of each bump. Remember to start the turn around one bump as early as you can, like skiing in a race course. Use the sides of the next bump like the walls of a bobsled run. Usually, they're not as tracked as the gullies, and the snow stays softer — better for making the turn.

• The third method is skiing in the troughs — the fastest line and the most aggressive. Practice this with a stem turn until you can do it parallel.

I encourage upper-level students to pick a line and, keeping a consistent shape and rhythm, to turn regardless of where the bump lies. This way, they incorporate all the tactics into one bump run.

Work with the terrain, don't fight it. Copper Mountain instructor Sarah Persson shares a trick she learned about skiing bumps during her ski racing days in Sweden: "I couldn't get it because the bumps were too much like a race course with pressure to turn in a certain place." Then one evening, skiing home in the dark after a few beers, she went over the children's rolling terrain. Relaxed, her loose legs slid up and over the bumps effortlessly like a roller coaster hugging its track. It felt so good, she went back to do it again.

Pole plant

Bump skiing requires a solid pole plant. Plant the pole on top of the bump, directly down the fall line, as though you were reaching for a door handle. As you move forward, move your body "through" the door. Then, get ready to open the next door with the other hand.

The shape of the turn, combined with a strong pole plant and an open body position, pave the way to good bump skiing.

Donna Weinbrecht — Who can forget her graceful flawless skiing through the bumps, with her long blond hair flying, in her first gold medal run at the 1992 Olympics? This Grace Kelly of skiing

---

made an imprint in the hearts and minds of women everywhere and remains a role model to this day. The four-time World Cup champion and winner of 33 World Cup titles — the same number won by Italian superstar Alberto Tomba — shares her secrets on bump technique and offers words of encouragement.

• You need good flat-skiing skills. If you have one bad habit in the flats, it will be 10 times more exaggerated in the moguls because things happen a lot faster. So practice your flat skiing!

• When learning, pick spread-out bumps, not tight ones. To learn speed control, slowly go up and over some of the bumps and feel the absorption with your legs. Practice turning up, turning down, turning in-between.

• Everything happens underneath the hips. Keep your feet underneath you. You don't want to reach with your feet because your buttocks will stay in back. A lot of women like to break at the waist, but you need to be *on top* of your skis. Let your legs come up underneath you [as you rise onto the bump], then push down [as you carve the backside], controlling your speed.

• Never ski on a 'platform.' If you do, your knees will be locked. Even though it looks like a platform, the knees are dynamic in successful bump skiing. It's a series of independent motions. When you go up, you want to push into the turn. You don't want to tuck the knee.

• The pole plant in bump skiing swings out — you hit, punch, break forward with the wrist — your arms never come down. Pole plant early in bump skiing.

• The eyes are important. Knowing and reading the terrain lets you know how you want to go over it. Ski on the offense, not defense.

• Go out there and have fun! You've got to put in the miles and get feedback from yourself ... Learn why one run is better than the last. Learn what makes a run smoother. Ask yourself why you could link turns better this time — maybe you didn't get in the back seat once. *You've* got to be your own best teacher. No one is always going to be around to tell you. But don't be too critical of yourself.

• Get in classes. Work on the basics. Analyze your own runs. Learn from yourself. You can't do the same thing over and over if you want to improve. Try to make a change.

• Observe other people who ski well. I didn't have a coach — I watched competitors. There were times I would get really round across the hill when I wanted to go more down the fall line and absorb. I wanted to know how to control my speed that way.

(CBS newscaster) Paula Zahn sked me about that. I thought it was a real high-level question. I guess there are a lot of people out there who want to know!

Powder

Freak out time! My panic button used to light up whenever I encountered powder, until I learned to relax and not fight it. When I could relax, acquiring the moves was easy. It will be easy for you too.

Jo Garuccio, a world champion masters triathlete, teaches skiing at Snowbird, Utah. She is a PSIA instructor trainer/examiner of the Intermountain Division and holds the position of assistant education vice president of the division. Jo shows us why skiing powder ranks as the ultimate ski experience and how you, too, can revel in its magic:

You went to bed with the wind and snow raging past your window and awoke to a winter wonderland — 18 inches of new fluff. Powder! Openly, you hope for it but secretly, you worry that you can't ski it. You wonder why people spend thousands of dollars looking for untracked snow in the Canadian Rockies or Utah's backcountry. What are "face shots," anyway, and how do you get them? Is skiing powder really ecstasy?

Yes! Nothing compares to floating rhythmically through two feet of powder, snow spraying in your face at every turn, the tassel of your hat the only thing visible above the fluff. Or sailing on boot-top deep silk over a smooth, packed surface. Or designing Figure 8 tracks like you see on posters. Wouldn't it be great if you could make your own?

Skiing powder is a legal drug — an effortless, addictive sensation that you must try! Before shedding light on the frenzy many people feel on powder days, let me dispel a few popular myths about skiing powder.

Myth One: Sitting back.

Many people still think powder skiing requires you to sit back on your skis. Unless you possess bionic legs, or you plan to ski only the first two hours of the day, you don't want to sit back. You should stay centered with your hips, knees and ankles in line over your feet as a base of support. Once in a while, snow will be heavy enough to force you to apply a little heel leverage, but this differs from keeping your knees at a 90-degree angle.

Myth Two: Skiing powder is a completely different technique than skiing packed snow.

Not so! A few modifications or slight changes in blending skills are necessary, but with good instruction, versatile skiers with strong skills can easily adapt to powder snow.

Myth Three: All powder is created equal.

Not every storm drops perfectly dry, light powder requiring nothing more than minimum effort to ski — not even in Utah's Little Cottonwood Canyon, touted as the ultimate powder-snow experience in the United States. If powder becomes more difficult to ski one day than the day before, that doesn't mean you've forgotten everything you've learned. Sometimes, certain powder conditions require more work. So go easy on your self-esteem!

Myth Four: Women are not strong enough to ski deep snow.

Strength and weight may be a factor in some conditions, but they're not a reason to hang up your skis on powder mornings. Women who are good technical skiers often outlast guys who ski with less finesse and more brute force. Heavy snow may bounce a lightweight person around a bit more but you can compensate by being more accurate with your movements.

Myth Five: Real women don't ski wide-body skis.

Nonsense! Don't let technology pass you by. When you see deep snow once every five years when your ski vacation happens to fall during a wet weather pattern, don't pass up the opportunity. Wide-body skis float in powder much better than conventional skis and require little speed to initiate a turn. They also help control speed, slowing you as you turn your feet across the hill. It's as easy as walking. Do yourself a favor on your next powder day. Find a ski shop that rents or demos the new, wider boards and learn the magic of skiing on powder.

Mastering the medium

If you suffer from bad habits on packed snow, those habits will be worse on powder. In fact, you may not even realize your basic technique needs improving until you experience a frustrating day in a foot of new snow. Take lessons. Take one before the powder arrives and more during or after the snowfall. If you sign up for a private lesson, ask for a Level II or Level III PSIA certified instructor. Do not rely on a husband or boyfriend to teach you to ski the soft stuff. It could mean the end of the relationship!

Balance

Balance stands alone as the most important factor in any sport. In powder snow, you must remain centered over your base of support. Sitting back will only make you tired and more prone to hurting yourself.

Balance involves active movement in the direction of the new turn. The "up" that instructors talk about doesn't mean vertical movement. It means extending your legs and moving your center of mass (lead by your belt buckle) toward the new turn.

Gravity can be helpful, relieving your muscles from solely dictating turn initiation — especially important for smaller people with smaller muscle mass. If you move vertically, you need to twist your feet more forcefully or use excessive upper body rotation to start the turn. In deep snow, such maneuvers can be detrimental and very tiring. When you move downhill with your center of mass, you hold a better chance of remaining balanced over your feet. If you don't move in the direction of the new turn, your skis will leave you behind and you'll end up sitting back.

Pole action influences balance significantly. Keep your hands within your peripheral vision. If your arms drop back, your hips and shoulders will, too. As you near the completion of the old turn, visualize the path your skis will take in the new turn. Swing your pole (a wrist and forearm movement only) toward the middle to end of that path and face your belt buckle in the same direction. If your pelvis and upper body face the new turn ready to move, you'll be less likely to hesitate or shop for another spot.

Turning

You need more momentum and progressive steering of your legs and feet when you're skiing in powder. You can't turn as abruptly as you can on packed snow. So be patient and glide more at the top of the turn, whether you initiate in a parallel stance or by stemming. As you feel momentum build, you can glide across the hill.

Edging

Don't be fooled by people who tell you to ski a completely flat ski in powder. Without a little tipping, the edges will catch and bury you quickly. You must learn to feather your edges and be progressive with edging movements. Don't overedge — your skis will shoot forward rapidly and require more muscle to steer once you initiate a direction change. Push your skis and feet into the snow as you guide them through the arc. Try to feel a snow bank build up to the outside of your skis as you push snow away from you as you shape the turn.

Unweighting

Lighten both skis simultaneously with a slight rise toward the new turn. Actively transferring weight from one ski to another results in one ski floating and one sinking into the powder. Your skis will also seek different directions. In shallow powder above a smooth, firm surface, you can get away with an active weight transfer.

Practice simultaneous unweighting on packed snow by not lifting your inside ski in a turn. This exercise teaches patience and finesse. You still feel a passive weight transfer as soon as you flatten the old outside ski and release the old outside edge. It's not necessary to step to the new ski. Simply get off the old one and steer both ski tips downhill. This works for stem turns as well.

Advanced skiers get enough speed and energy from the snow to retract their feet slightly to make the skis light. This retraction may be combined with a slight rise. If the skier is traveling fast, a slight retraction may be enough.

Terrain and powder type

When powder piles up light and airy on top of a smooth, packed surface, sample it on any green, blue or black slope. Any technique variation works — until the snow gets significantly tracked by skiers. Variable conditions add another dimension to powder and make things a bit tougher. Heavy or very deep powder requires a slightly steeper slope than what you usually ski in order to gain speed to move through it.

Be kind to yourself. If you've never skied powder, start on slopes groomed before and during the storm. This snow won't be as deep as ungroomed snow on black diamonds. As you gain confidence, you can progress to the bottomless stuff.

Above all, ski safe and obey posted signs. Never ski alone. (Buy a set of powder cords, lightweight leashes that attach to your skis. They cost bout $10. To order, call (916) 926-2600; FAX (800) 926-9904. Without cords, you run the risk of searching for a buried ski for hours. And don't expect help. There are no friends, husbands or boyfriends on a powder day!)

Steeps
Steep slopes, especially steep slopes with bumps, a.k.a. double black diamonds, present more challenge than most women want in their repertoire of skiing. But nothing proves more satisfying than completing a steep run standing on your feet!

Jamie Mackintosh, an instructor at Jackson Hole, bases this advice and inspiring thoughts on her own experience skiing the steeps as well as teaching others the technique.

To successfully ski the steeps, you must blend the right combinations of ski technique and mental attitude. All the skill and aptness in the world won't help if you can't hold it together mentally and trust your movements when the slopes begin to get steeper.

Steep is a relative term. It can mean a black-diamond run in the Poconos of Pennsylvania, a yellow "!" caution chute at Jackson Hole or a 60-degree couloir in Alaska's Chugach Range. Wherever the mountain, the technique for skiing it remains the same:

• Stand centered over your feet. Focus on the arch of your foot as a good point of balance.

• Press firmly against your inside edge. A sturdy edgeset is crucial.

- Project your torso, shoulders and hips down the fall line.
- Keep your hands out in front. You need to reach down and forward with a strong, aggressive pole plant.
- Dynamically retain your balance while you make a complete turn. Anticipate where your skis will go. The steeper the terrain, the faster the fall line.
- Keep your wits about you!

As you would when running or walking down a steep slope, control your direction and speed with turn shape (see "Skiing in Control"). Keep moving. Momentum, properly directed, can help you ski with fluency.

The ability to release your edges and steer your skis equals in importance the ability to set your edges and stop your skis. Skiing the steeps can be like walking on a balance beam. Precision counts!

Keep things in perspective: one turn at a time. Pace yourself to ski the entire run or a section at a time. Don't stand at the top and freeze, staring at the bottom. Get moving and keep moving. Don't stop in the middle of a pitch where you can't be seen, or where you block other skiers' lines. Stop only in safe, clear zones. And don't overlook the danger of another skier overtaking you or, if you're in the back country, the threat of avalanches.

When skiing chutes, observe these rules of common sense and courtesy:
- Ski the chute and clear it.
- Allow the skiers ahead of you to do the same.

• Check out steep routes from the bottom before attempting to ski them. Obstacles can be hidden from above in the same way the backside of a mogul is not visible to the approaching skier. Although the chute may be free, rocks and other debris can litter the runouts.

• A fall usually precedes a long slide that can pick up speed and send you careening out of control into another skier or object.

• If you fall, try to arrest your slide by swinging your legs below your body and then digging in your edges. This not only stops you, but protects your arms and head from being a battering ram and places you in a better position on the hill to stand up. If your skis release, dig in the heels or edges of your ski boots.

Much of the fear of steeps exists because of the possible consequences. While these consequences represent reality, we can reduce the risk factors significantly by being prepared. Start with the building blocks of believing you can do it and being there because you want to be. Try to maintain good mental and physical balance. Gradually extend your comfort zone. Don't push the envelope too far in any direction all at once.

I have seen more people with lower-level skills and the right attitude survive steep skiing than I have good skiers lacking confidence. I have also found skiers on steep slopes with heads big enough to get them there but skills grossly too inadequate to get them down. This places them in a dangerous — and unnecessary — situation. It's like trying to eat hot soup with your fingers.

Given all the consequences, skiing the steeps can be a rewarding, successful event in a well-assessed situation with knowledgeable participants. Steep skiing provides the greatest challenges in this lifetime sport with real-life experiences.

Racing to improve technique

Everyone associates racing with speed and competition, two things that turn many women off in skiing. But have you ever thought of running gates to improve technique and inject a little spice in your skiing?

Brenda Buglione competed on the World Cup circuit for the U.S. Ski Team and raced on the Women's Pro Tour for six years. She explains how racing can improve skiing technique for recreational skiers.

Balance

By now you know that good balance on your skis is a prerequisite for skiing. The athletic stance prepares you for quick action, and anticipates upcoming slalom gates, moguls or quick turns on the steeps.

Running slalom forces you to maintain this balanced stance — poor body position makes it nearly impossible to negotiate gates. A racer's weight must be forward and pressuring the inside edge of the downhill ski in order for it to carve on the correct line around the gates. A tendency to lean back on the tails of the skis pulls the weight to the heels and prevents pressure at the center of the skis.

Anticipating and adjusting to the steepness of the slope also helps maintain balance. You must always position yourself at a right angle to the hill. For example, if you are standing on a flat slope, you are at 90 degrees to the hill. But as the hill gets steeper, to maintain that 90 degrees you must project your body forward.

Counter Rotation — facing down the hill

Skiing gates forces you to maintain a disciplined position with no upper-body rotation. Rotating your upper body and hips causes the tails of your skis to slide and hinders the ski's ability to carve a turn.

Your upper body and hips must face down the fall-line, with your shoulders level and legs moving underneath. This counter-rotated position keeps pressure on the inside downhill edge, enhancing edge control. Skiing gates teaches you to turn your body away from the gates and prevents your weight from falling to the uphill ski.

Pole plants

In racing, movements must coincide so that no motion is wasted. The pole plant should be kept to simple wrist action. Extraneous arm movement takes the weight off the downhill ski — forcing you off balance — and makes finishing a slalom course difficult. A solid pole plant in front brings the hips forward at the beginning of every turn and positions your weight where it can edge and pressure the ski. By focusing on this simplicity and using the pole plant as a timing device, you'll find it easier to maintain balance and initiate turns.

Fast feet

Skiing gates forces you to make edge-to-edge turns quicker than you would free skiing. No matter how fast or slow you ski, in a race course you must turn when the gates dictate, instead of where you think you want to turn. At first, this might be difficult but with practice you'll find your ability to move your feet quickly and anticipate the next turn will improve. Developing these skills is beneficial when you need to avoid natural obstacles like rocks or icy patches or other skiers. You'll gain confidence knowing you can turn quickly and precisely to control speed or negotiate challenging terrain.

Timing and line

Learning to recognize the correct line through the gates helps you make perfectly carved, comma-shaped turns. When turning in the gates, you must make the direction change at the top of the turn, where gravity and centrifugal force works with you. If you point your skis straight at the pole and wait to edge at the end of the turn, the turn takes the shape of a "J" and increased speed will force you off the line and out of the gates.

Knowing how to change direction early in the turn helps you stay in control and keep your line when free skiing down a steep, icy slope.

Lisa Feinberg Densmore competed on the Women's Pro Ski Racing Tour from 1984 to 1990. A member of the U. S. Masters Alpine Ski Team, Lisa offers this insight on ski racing.

Fear

Racing helps alleviate the fear factor. As your technique improves, you become more confident in a course and on the open slopes, raising your fear threshold high enough to handle any skiing.

Many women feel insecure when terrain gets steeper or rougher than their comfort level. When you ski gates, each course deteriorates a little more with each run, to slicker ice or deeper ruts. You get accustomed *gradually* to the tougher conditions during a gate-training session, instead of bouncing from a perfectly groomed slope to trouble. After running gates a while, smooth slopes in free skiing seem easy, the rugged slopes less rugged. (There's not much difference between a rut next to a gate and a trough between moguls.)

Though you may be unsure about going fast, once you've experienced a timed run such as a NASTAR course, you may find it hard not to go back to try for a personal best. Suddenly, you feel a *need* for speed!

New challenge

Ski racing can rekindle the challenge and excitement of the slopes. Skiers who have mastered the basics can lose interest in skiing, especially if their regular mountain is small and groomed like a carpet. But racers can ski the same trail a hundred times and still be challenged because every course is different. Skiers who want the thrill of speed find the race arena the only place on the mountain where they can ski fast without the ski patrol breathing down their neck.

You can find ski racing virtually at all ski areas. Some programs run in a series during the season from one resort to another. Others, like NASTAR, are offered daily. Still others are single events. Costs vary.

Adult recreational racing programs

NASTAR (**NA**tional **STA**ndard **R**ace) was offered at 180 ski areas in 32 states during the 1993-94 ski season, which marked NASTAR's 25th anniversary.
- Race format: Giant Slalom.
- Open to: any skier, any age, any abilities.
- How it works: Racers earn gold, silver and bronze medals based on age, sex and a unique handicap system, which compares the racer's time with members of the U.S. Ski Team. State and national leaders earn awards and prizes and national winners are listed in *SKI* magazine.
- Information: World Wide Sports, 402D, AABC, Aspen, C0 81611; (303) 925-7864; FAX (303) 925-7882.

United States Ski Association offers two recreational racing programs:

Masters Racing attracts skiers who are *serious* about racing as well as former collegiate, professional and U.S. Ski Team racers.
- Race format: Slalom, Giant Slalom, Super G, Downhill.
- Open to: Ages 18 and older.

- How it works: Competitors ski in age classifications in local season-long series to qualify for national and international championship races.

Citizens Racing is mostly for city folks who ski recreationally on weekends.

- Race format: Slalom, Giant Slalom.
- Open to: Ages 21 and older; all abilities.
- How it works: Participants are grouped according to age and ability. Top citizen racers from each region attend U.S. championships. The winners there represent the United States in "Citadin" competition in Europe.

For more information on USSA racing: United States Ski Association, Recreation Programs, P.O. Box 100, Park City, UT 84060; (801) 649-9090.

Mitsubushi Motors Diamond Ski Classic is a U.S. Recreational Ski Association program offered in six regions throughout the season to members of the association (non-members pay a small fee). It emphasizes *fun* in ski racing.

- Race format: Dual Giant Slalom
- Open to: All ages and abilities.
- How it works: Participants ski two runs in the novice, intermediate or elite class. Their best time goes toward accumulating points. Highest-point winners win a trip to the finals.

For more information: 1315 Gene Autry Way, Anaheim, CA 92805; (714) 634-1050.

Pay-to-Race courses (formerly called Marlboro Ski Challenge) operate daily at all major resorts.

- Race format: Dual Giant Slalom.

- Open to: All ages, all abilities.
- How it works: Buy tokens for $1 at starting gate; race as many times as you want. Race times displayed at finish line after each run.

Charity racing

Race courses continue to be successful venues for charities to raise money. Many invite a celebrity or two from the sports and entertainment fields and draw huge crowds who pay big bucks to ski with the likes of Christie Brinkley, Nicollette Sheridan and Clint Eastwood. These annual races at various resorts are fun and low-key (for most people!) and usually include lots of social events and media hype.

Jimmie Heuga's Mazda Ski Express raises about $1 million for the Jimmie Heuga Center's medical program and research activities for multiple sclerosis. The season-long series spans 18 states, with national finals held in Vail.

- Race format: Dual Giant Slalom and four-hour marathon.
- Open to: All ages. Each three-person team must be co-ed.
- How it works: Scoring is based half on the amount of pledges raised, a quarter on vertical feet skied in the marathon, and a quarter on combined times of each team. At the finals, each member of the top fund-raising team wins a Mazda.

For more information: PO Box 5919, Avon, CO 81620; (800) 367-3101 or (303) 949-7172.

Chapter Summary:

Don't freak out on the hard stuff. P.S.I.A. instructors Christie Smith, Alison Clayton, Barbara Sanders, Jo Garuccio and Jamie Mackintosh tell us how to turn 'em on ice, bumps, steeps, and in powder, and teach how to do it in control.

Donna Weinbrecht, 1992 Olympic gold medalist, shares her tips for skiing bumps, and racers Brenda Buglione and Lisa Feinberg Densmore show us how running gates improves free skiing.

Chapter Thirteen

Women to women

"Lessons are great! They give you hints and tips to control your skis and make skiing more challenging and enjoyable. I like the self-confidence I get from this knowledge."

— Anonymous, age 35 from Colorado

"I'd like to look smooth, in control, and happy through the moguls. Great instruction is the only way I know to get there."

— Anonymous, age 63 from New York

"It helps to have an instructor tell me what to do instead of my husband."

— Irene, age 66, from Wisconsin

Academics are taking a second look at new research showing that boys demand, and get, teachers' attention more than girls in grade school through grad school. But remove the boys from the classroom and girls are more likely to participate in discussions, to achieve more and to hold themselves higher in self-esteem, the studies show.

The concept also has proven effective in ski schools. The trend toward all-women ski classes is

---

snowballing in the ski industry. According to the Denver-based National Ski Areas Association, nearly half of its more than 300 ski-area members now offer some type of women-only instructional program.

Chicks on Sticks, Babes on Boards, Thelma and Louise on Skis, call them what you may — participants of these clinics know a good thing when they ski it.

• Liz from Seattle explained why she enrolled in a women's ski seminar at Breckenridge: "In class I can ask questions freely because the female instructors *listen*. Men instructors don't seem to be in touch with how women feel about skiing. It (women's ski seminar) gives me confidence to ski with men back home."

• Vicky, a tennis coach from Denver, was attending her fourth women's ski clinics. "You don't have that macho thing you get in classes with men," she said.

• Ellyn, a teacher from Chicago, noticed an absence of "that male-female competition and comparing" of mixed classes.

• Stephanie, a rugby player from New York, came to a women's seminar at Copper Mountain because she found "male instructors gear their teaching toward men in coed classes — and they never address the fear factor."

Remember the differences between men's and women's approaches to skiing that we talked about in Chapter One? Men want to "Rambo" down the hill; women take it slower, concentrating more on technique. And how can we forget that man on the lift who yelled "Go faster!" at the woman neatly weaving down a mogul field!

All-women ski classes remove the pressure to be as aggressive as men. Women learn at their own pace, in their own way. With everyone sharing the same goals and strategies, the class becomes an ideal learning environment. It breeds success.

Telluride Ski School Director Annie Vareille-Savath says all-women classes work because most women are not as confident about their athletic ability as men. "In coed classes, women tend to ski defensively, and lose quality," Vareille-Savath says. "But competition on the same level pushes them to be better and builds confidence.

"We show women how to accomplish goals, how to recognize and deal with fears and to coordinate mind and body," Vareille-Savath says. "What they learn skiing, they carry throughout their lives. It's better than psychotherapy!"

Former Olympic downhill racer Holly Flanders directs the Ladies Ski Adventure at Park City, Utah. She says she believes the workshops help women get psyched for skiing, especially women who feel hesitant about hitting the slopes.

The programs owe much of their success to the quality of instruction. Ski schools select the *crème de la crème* of their fully-certified women instructors well-versed in the latest teaching methods and equipment technology, and capable of setting examples in a non-condescending way. And their skiing definitely presents a visual, achievable model. At Heavenly in California's Lake Tahoe Region, most of the women instructors in the three-day seminars also hold certification in aerobics and fitness. New Hampshire's Waterville Valley's long-weekend women's programs include coaching from racers on the Women's Pro Ski Tour during the tour's scheduled stop there.

Besides mastery of skills and building confidence, women come for the sheer fun of it. The multi-day seminars can be a slumber party-sorority house-Girl Scout-camp rolled into one great getaway. "Let's Do Lunch" takes on a whole new meaning: Picture a sun-drenched mountaintop deck where new friends celebrate their skiing breakthroughs over a flask of wine (or flasks, depending on how many breakthroughs they're celebrating). The name Women's Ski Esprit, chosen for its women's programs by California's Snow Summit ski area, captures the spirit of camaraderie that sets these clinics apart. The joviality extends to the instructors, too. Jonathan Lohnes, ski school director of Timberline Ski Area on Mt. Hood in Oregon, says during the first year of one-day women's workshops the instructors enjoyed "a fabulous experience teaching the participants."

The experience even can be cathartic. Wendy Nevins, an instructor of women's seminars in Aspen, says emotions get caught up in our muscles. "When we begin to focus on our bodies, what's happening in our minds sometimes spills out." Then the bonding really gets tight.

A few years ago when I was in Crested Butte, Colorado, Kim Reichhelm invited me to sample one day of her four-day women's ski program, Women's Ski Adventures, in mid-session. When the class broke for lunch, Kim apologetically explained that I wouldn't be returning for the afternoon. She said the women in the class felt that a stranger in their midst interfered with their cohesion and diluted the quality of instruction. Understanding the dynamics of these clinics, I agreed to leave peaceably!

One-day clinics

Women's ski programs range from one-day clinics to all-inclusive, multi-day vacation packages. Some single-day workshops are held on a once-a-week, consecutive-day schedule, like the six-out-of-eight-week seminar hosted by Idaho's Schweitzer Mountain Resort. Others operate on a specific date, like Winter Park's Women's Early Season Clinic in December and Women's Mid-Season Clinic in March.

One-day clinics vary greatly in price and length. Some offer a few hours of instruction; others run all day. Many include lunch, an après-ski party or an indoor presentation. Video analysis, an important tool for learning to ski, often is part of these lessons. Deer Valley's Weekly Winter Escape for Women in Utah includes fitness and nutrition discussions and ski races in the afternoon. Whatever you choose, be sure you know whether a lift ticket is included in the price.

Other programs, sometimes called Ladies Day, promote discounts on lift tickets, lessons and equipment rentals for women, but they don't offer women-to-women instruction. New York's Catamount ski area offers discounted lift tickets to women, free child care and free lessons in *coed* classes during the week. Kudos to them for getting women out of the house and on the mountain, but I think they're missing the point. When I asked why the ski school didn't teach women-only classes, a man in the office said, "I wouldn't know how to do that!"

Multi-day clinics

Multi-day sessions run from two- or three-day workshops to longer ski "weeks," which usually run five to six days. Among the most exclusive is Beaver Creek's Technique Weeks for Women, a complete ski vacation at the posh Hyatt Regency. The price, about $1,475 for one person booking double occupancy, includes lift tickets, four days' instruction with video, indoor learning sessions, five nights' lodging, daily breakfasts, opening and closing dinners, and a sponsor's gift such as a Bogner sweater or duffel bag.

Participants receive a helpful Before You Go guide including suggestions on everything from clothes to conditioning. The ski-in, ski-out hotel features a health spa, restaurants and "ski valets" who deliver your skis and boots every morning and whisk them away at the end of the day!

Two- and three-day clinics, like California's Northstar-at-Tahoe Women's Ski Clinic, offer fewer days on the slopes but rank just as high in quality of instruction. For less than $200, you get three all-day lessons and lift tickets, video critique and an après-ski party with a talk from a sports psychologist. Lodging is not included.

Ideally, you should reserve your place in a women's ski seminar weeks, even months, in advance. Call the resort's main number and ask for the ski school. (Most U.S. and Canadian ski resorts offering these seminars are listed with phone numbers at the end of this chapter.) Request a seminar brochure for all the information you need. Often, you or your travel agent can book everything at once: lodging, lift tickets, seminar reservation, car and equipment rentals.

Some clinics offer optional activities like snowboarding, snowmobiling, race clinics, cross-country skiing, heli-skiing, and (as mentioned in Chapter Nine) "climbing the wall" at Telluride's Women's Week. These can be thrilling, once-in-a-lifetime adventures, or the impetus for learning another winter sport!

If you consider yourself an awesome expert skier, there's a place for you, too, in women's ski seminars. Instructors will fine-tune your skiing and provide you plenty of challenges on the most difficult terrain on the mountain — places you may never have skied. And, you'll be skiing with some of the best women skiers in the world!

Colorado's Ski Cooper offers a specialized clinic called Women in Powder for the "promising and progressive" woman skier. In two days (including one day of snowcat skiing) instructors avow you'll be able to ski powder and enjoy it!

Women who have never skied may need to look harder for women-only classes: many programs accept only skiers who have reached advanced-beginner or lower-intermediate level. Check this if you are just beginning to ski, or haven't skied since you began years ago, and want the advantage of learning with other women. If you can't find one that accepts never-evers, call a small, local ski area. Because of their less intimidating size and friendly atmospheres, these areas that specialize in learn-to-ski programs are perfect for beginning skiing. Colorado's SilverCreek Ski Area is one such place — they even initiated a women-only, beginner-only clinic as a springboard for more advanced women's programs.

At the clinic

When you arrive, you are placed in a small class, usually no more than six women, according to your ability. (Some clinics send out questionnaires to determine your level prior to your arrival; others assess your skiing ability on the first morning.) If you find yourself in a group that skis slower than you, or one more advanced, speak with your instructor. She will be more than willing to move you to another group. Instructors bend over backward to make these experiences rewarding and *fun*.

Instruction is only as good as the instructor. Any time you're dissatisfied, complain to the ski school or clinic director. If you think there's a problem, say so early enough in the session to reap the benefits of another instructor or class.

Many of the bad instructor stories I hear involve ski classes in Europe. There, instructors don't really teach; they act more like guides who say, "Follow me," and ski off in front of the class, which is supposed to copy him. (Male instructors teach adult students; usually women are assigned only children's classes.) One California woman wrote in my survey: "In Europe, I improved radically because ski instructors are very strict and hit you with their poles!" Another recalls how her instructor skied off into the fog, never to be seen again!

Small wonder European women laud American ski schools and love the idea of women's ski clinics, which only now are beginning to take shape in Europe. I know of two: at Méribel, in Les Trois Vallées in France; and at Châtel, also in France in the Portes du Soleil region on the border with Switzerland.

Women-only ski instruction began in the United States with Elissa Slanger's Women's Way, held at Squaw Valley, California in 1975. Copper Mountain picked up the concept a few years later and the idea began to flourish.

Breckenridge Women Ski Seminar instructor Jan Degerberg sums up one of the reasons for the seminars' success: "The approach instructors use in teaching can make it or break it for women. A 22-year-old macho kid instructor who wants to 'go for it,' teaching a nervous woman who hasn't skied in 12 years could be a negative situation."

Could be?

It's always better when a woman is compatible with her instructor, Degerberg says.

The nature of learning

As a consultant in Sports Science for Copper Mountain Ski School, Neil Wolkodof knows how to get the most from ski instruction. Here he tells us the ingredients needed for making skiing improvements possible.

Lessons are not always a guarantee of learning to ski better. In fact, a lesson will provide the necessary information and techniques, *but your mental state will dictate whether the learning is effective.* In essence, if you learn *how* to learn, you can keep improving your ski techniques long after your lessons are over. Lessons and clinics tend to put people in a learning mode where change is supported but not guaranteed. In either situation, your mind-set will determine the ultimate results.

The first key to learning a new skill or refining an old one is to understand the nature of learning. This is difficult to determine because studies cannot directly access the neurological pathways, but we can make some very good observations and derive some principles based on learning examples, situations and experiments.

Learning involves three phases:
- Understanding the skill.
- Practicing the skill.
- Making that skill automatic so that movements and reactions occur without conscious thinking.

Applying this model of learning to skiing will result in drastically improving your rate of learning.

Understanding

The understanding or *cognitive* phase of learning means getting an idea of what you are trying to accomplish. This involves knowing what you currently do in a given situation, like skiing bumps, vs. what is optimum. You can understand information *visually* (watching the instructor), *auditorily* (listening to the description of the action and making a mental picture), or *kinesthetically* (how a movement feels). While visual information provides more details about the movement goal and intricacies, not everyone is set up to learn visually. The key is to determine your preferred style of information reception.

Many people don't learn because they don't have an image of what needs to be accomplished. If you don't have a goal or understanding, you probably won't improve. Your goal should be to pick one or two points of information that will lead to performing or improving the skill. For example, "Press on your right ski to turn left." Information should be specific.

Practicing

After you gain an understanding of the movement, the next phase is practicing, or the *associative* phase. This is the most critical phase because you begin to develop new motor pathways. In the case of old skills being refined, you are attempting to change or develop new muscle memory.

There are several methods you can use to make this phase effective. Learning best takes place when you slow down. In order to do this, you should pick terrain and speed that is below your normal ability. If you normally ski "black" moguls, practice on a blue run with consistent bumps to improve mogul technique. In this phase of learning, you must actively try to establish each movement. Don't think about the terrain or speed not being at your maximum ability level.

This phase reminds us that learning is active and requires a good deal of mental effort. It also shows us that the quality of the movements and not the quantity is the prime determinant of whether you begin to learn the skill. Better to make 10 good linked bump turns than 20 wrong ones. In this phase, it is good to remind yourself to do what the instructor said, like to press or to reach. In this phase you need to link actively the desired movements with the trigger or stimulus.

Automatic

Once the skill is fully learned, this approach works well. But fully developing a skill takes the *active thinking* required to associate movement with a stimulus. Once the active thinking produces the desired results, the automatic approach kicks in.

Most people feel they don't think at all during this phase, but in actuality you *are* thinking, just with different parameters. Sports thinking can be characterized as *visual* rather than verbal thinking. You simply think in pictures, use those pictures to cue actions, and go on to the next movement. You are aware and in control, just not in the same sense as when verbally thinking during the associative phase.

The biggest error most people make in the automatic phase is to think and cue information verbally rather than visually. This leads to slow and/or inaccurate movements and, sometimes, just total disaster. Enter "Close Encounters of the Third Pine" when skiing. You can slowly enter the zone of visual thinking by taking movements you have perfected and applying them to slightly more challenging situations — steeper terrain, bigger bumps, deeper powder.

There is a time to think verbally and a time to think visually. Learning requires active, and in many cases verbal, thinking to develop new movements. In this case, a few good turns are worth many bad turns. As you evolve to the performance or the automatic mode, you must make those thinking patterns more and more visual in order to make fully the transition to performance. And when you think, think positive!

Chapter Summary:

Women-only ski clinics are popping up at North American ski areas in great numbers. Women say when the intimidation and competition of men is removed, they learn to ski better and, sometimes, even have more fun! These women-teaching-women classes have proven to be the ideal learning environment for women in skiing.

Neil Wolkodof offers tips on how people learn to ski.

Choose a women's ski program from the following list of more than 140 offered in North America.

U.S. and Canadian Ski Areas with Alpine Ski Programs for Women

This list was compiled from National Ski Areas Association and regional ski associations. With the increasing popularity of women's clinics, some may have been added to ski school offerings after this book's publication prior to the 1994-95 ski season. Areas with an asterisk (*) offer Jeannie Thoren's equipment clinics

Alaska

Alyeska Resort	(907) 783-1089
Eaglecrest Ski Area	(907) 790-2001

California

Alpine Meadows	(800) 441-4423
Heavenly	(800) 243-2836
Kirkwood	(209) 258-6000
Mammoth Mountain	(800) 832-7320
Mountain High	(619) 249-5808
Northstar-at-Tahoe	(800) 533-6787
Sierra-at-Tahoe	(916) 659-7453
Snow Summit	(909) 866-5766
Squaw Valley	(800) 545-4350
Sugar Bowl	(916) 426-3651

Colorado

Arapahoe Basin	(800) 255-3715
Aspen Mountain	(303) 923-1227
Beaver Creek Resort	(800) 323-4386
Breckenridge Ski Resort	(800) 789-7669
Ski Cooper	(719) 486-3684
Copper Mountain Resort	(800) 458-8386
Crested Butte Mountain Resort	(800) 992-7700
Eldora Mountain Resort	(303) 440-8700 ext. 225
Keystone	(800) 255-3715
Loveland Ski Area	(303) 571-5580
Monarch Ski Resort	(719) 539-3573
Powderhorn Ski Resort	(303) 268-5700

Purgatory-Durango Ski Resort	(303) 247-9000 ext. 5145
SilverCreek Ski Area	(800) 448-9458
Steamboat Ski Resort	(303) 879-6111
(*Snow Country* Ski School)	(800) 282-7656
Ski Sunlight	(303) 945-7491
Snowmass	(303) 923-1227
Telluride Ski Resort	(303) 728-4424
Vail (*Snow Country* Ski School)	(800) 282-7656
Winter Park Resort	(303) 726-5514 ext. 331
Wolf Creek	(303) 264-5639

Connecticut

Ski Sundown	(203) 379-9851

Idaho

Schweitzer Mountain Resort	(800) 831-8810
Sun Valley	(208) 622-2231

Illinois

*Alpine Valley	(800) 227-9395 ext. 461
Chestnut Mountain Resort	(800) 397-1320

Maine

Sugarloaf USA	(800) 843-5623
Sunday River Ski Resort	(800) 543-2754

Massachusetts

Jiminy Peak	(413) 738-5500
Nashoba Valley Ski Area	(508) 692-3033
Wachusett Mountain	(508) 464-2300

Michigan

*Ski Brule Mountain	(906) 265-4957
*Indianhead Mountain Resort	(906) 229-5181
*Marquette Mountain	(906) 225-1155
The Homestead Resort	(616) 334-5000

Minnesota

*Buck Hill Ski Area	(612) 435-7174
*Giants Ridge	(800) 688-7669
*Mount Frontenac	(612) 388-5826
*Powder Ridge Ski Area	(800) 348-7734
*Spirit Mountain	(800) 642-6377
Welch Village Ski Area	(800) 203-0406
*Wild Mountain Ski Area	(800) 447-4958

Montana

The Big Mountain	(406) 862-3511
Bridger Bowl	(406) 587-2111
Discovery Basin	(406) 563-2184
Great Divide	(406) 449-3746
Lost Trail	(406) 821-3702
Maverick Mountain	(406) 834-3454
Montana Snowbowl	(406) 549-9777
Red Lodge Mountain	(406) 446-2610

Nevada

Diamond Peak Ski Resort	(702) 832-1177

New Hampshire

Attitash Ski Area	(603) 374-2368
The Balsams/Wilderness	(800) 255-0600 U.S./CN
	(800) 255-0800 NH
Cannon Mountain	(603) 823-5563
Gunstock Area	(800) 486-7862
Loon Mountain	(603) 745-8111 ext. 5682
Mt. Sunapee	(603) 763-2356
Waterville Valley	(603) 236-8311

New Jersey

Hidden Valley Ski Resort	(201) 764-6161
Craigmeur Ski Area	(201) 697-4500

New Mexico

Taos Ski Valley	(505) 776-2291

New York

Belleayre Mt. Ski Center	(914) 254-5600
Bristol Mountain Ski Resort	(716) 374-6000
Greek Peak	(800) 955-2754
Holiday Valley Resort	(716) 699-2345
*Lake Placid	(518) 946-2223
Toggenburg Ski Center	(315) 683-5842
Ski Valley	(716) 374-5157
Ski Windham	(518) 734-4300

North Carolina

Appalachian Ski Mountain	(704) 295-9312

Oregon

Anthony Lakes Mtn. Resort	(503) 963-4599
Mt. Bachelor Ski Resort	(800) 829-2442
Mt. Hood Meadows Ski Resort	(503) 337-2222
Timberline	(503) 231-5402
Willamette Pass	(800) 444-5030

Pennsylvania

Big Boulder Ski Area	(717) 722-0100
Jack Frost Mountain	(800) 443-8433
Whitetail Ski Resort	(717) 328-9400

Utah

Deer Valley Ski Resort	(800) 424-3337
Park City Ski Area	(800) 222-2754
Snowbird Ski Resort	(801) 742-2222
Solitude Ski Resort	(800) 748-4754

Vermont

Ascutney Mountain Resort	(802) 484-7711
Killington Ski Area	(800) 372-2007
Okemo Mountain Resort	(802) 228-4041
Smugglers' Notch	(802) 644-8851
Stratton Mountain	(800) 843-6867
Sugarbush	(802) 583-2381

Virginia

Massanutten Ski Resort   (800) 207-6277

Washington

Crystal Mountain Resort   (206) 663-2265
Ski Bluewood   (509) 382-4725
White Pass Ski Area   (509) 672-3100

Wisconsin

*Alpine Valley Resort   (414) 642-7374
*Cascade Mountain   (800) 992-2754
Mt. La Crosse Ski Area   (608) 788-0044
*Rib Mountain Ski Area   (715) 845-2846
*Sunburst Ski Area   (414) 626-8404
*Trollhaugen Ski Area   (715) 755-2955
*Whitecap Mountain   (800) 933-7669

Wyoming

Grand Targhee Ski Resort   (800) 827-4433
Jackson Hole Ski Resort   (307) 733-2292

Canada

Grouse Mountain, BC   (604) 984-0661
Lake Louise Ski Area, AB   (403) 522-3555
Mt. Louis-Moonstone, ON   (705) 835-2112
Panorama Resort, BC   (604) 342-6941
Searchmont Resort, ON   (705) 781-2340
Whistler Resort, BC   (800) 944-7853

Resources

Books

Aburdene, Patricia and Naisbitt, John. *Megatrends for Women*. New York, Random House, 1992.

Bailey, Covert and Bishop, Lea. *The Fit or Fat Woman: Solutions for Women's Unique Concerns*. Boston, Houghton Mifflin Co. 1989.

Briles, Judith. *The Confidence Factor: How Self-Esteem Can Change Your Life*. MasterMedia Limited, 1990.

Estés, Clarissaa Pinkola. *Women Who Run with the Wolves*. New York, Ballantine Books, 1992.

Gallwey, Timothy and Kriegel, Bob, *Inner Skiing*. New York, Random House, 1977.

Gray, John. *Men Are from Mars, Women Are from Venus*. New York, Harper Collins, 1992.

Leocha, Charles. *Skiing America* and *Ski Europe*, Boston, World Leisure Corporation, 1994.

Jeffers, Susan, PhD. *Feel the Fear and Do It Anyway*. New York, Ballantine Books, 1987.

Wells, Christine. *Women, Sport, & Performance: A Physiological Perspective*. (2nd ed.) Champaign, Ill., Human Kinetics Books, 1991.

Witherell, Warren and Evrard, David. *The Athletic Skier*. Salt Lake City, Utah, 1993.

(Used in the Women's Ski Discovery segment)

DeCoursey, Doug, and Linder, Darwyn, Ph.D. *Visual skiing, The Essential Mental and Physical Skills for the Modern Skier*. New York, Doubleday, 1990.

McCluggage, Denis. *The Centered Skier*. Waitsfield, Vermont, Tempest Books, 1992.

Porter, Kay, Ph.D., and Foster, Judy. *The Mental Athlete*. New York, Ballantine Books, 1987.

Video

Densmore, Lisa Feinberg. "BODY PREP! The Ultimate Ski Fitness Video." Hanover, N.H., Driscoll Communications, 1988.

"The Signature of Excellence." Stowe, Vt., Driscoll Communications, 1992.

Wade, Patty. "In Shape to Ski." Aspen Colo., 1993.

Magazine articles

Alberts, Nuna. "What Makes a Woman Happy?" *First for Women,* (December 13, 1993), p. 38.

Berger, Robert, M.D., "How To Protect Skin and Eyes on the Slopes," *Snow Country,* (March/April, 1993), p. 86.

"Buyers Guide." *SKI,* (September, 1993)

Cowan, Jay. "The Selective Eye." *SKI,* (September, 1993), pp. 195-198.

"Are Composites King?" *SKI,* (September, 1993), p. 189-190.

Curtin, Irwin. "America's Top Ski Shops." *Snow Country,* (January/February, 1994), p. 54.

Fry, John. "Put Women in Charge." *Snow Country,* (November, 1993), p. 8.

Hall, Julie K. "Fiber and Fabric Guide." *Ski Tech,* (October, 1993), pull-out section. "Skiwear for Real People, *Ski Tech,* (March, 1994), pp. 42-58.

Harb, Harold. "Body Alignment Relating to Biomechanics." *The Professional Skier,* (Fall, 1993), pp. 22-26. "1 Fix for 6 Common Errors." *Snow Country,* (January/February, 1994), pp. 104-112.

Hogen, Jackson. "Take Skis for a Demo Run Before Buying." *Snow Country,* (October, 1993), p. 116.

Howden, Michael. "9 Simple Steps to a Better Backshop." *Ski Tech,* (November/December, 1993), pp. 46-47.

Irons, Dave. "Testing 101." *Ski Tech,* (November/December, 1993), pp. 26-28.

Levine, Carol. "Physiological Considerations in Teaching Women to Ski." *The Professional Skier,* (Fall, 1993), pp. 14-18.

Masia, Seth. "Battle of the Flexes,"*SKI,* (September, 1993), pp. 174-175 "Movers and Shapers," *SKI,* (September, 1993), p. 78

Russelman, Bernadette. "Matters at Hand." *SKI,* (September, 1993), pp. 205-209.

Suplizio, Cindy and Hintermeister, Robert. "Do Anatomical and Physiological Differences Between Genders Affect Skiing?" *The Professional Skier,* (Fall, 1993), pp. 19-20, 62-63.

Ulmer, Kristen. "The Right to Ski to Die," *Skiing,* (November, 1993), p. 36, 217.

Wardlaw, Tait. "93-94 Ski Directory." *Ski Tech,* (September, 1993), pp. 40-55. "93-94 Boot & Binding Directory." *Ski Tech,* (October, 1993), pp. 55-64.

Newspapers

The Denver Post, July 18, 1994.

USA Today, Nov. 12, 1993; February 28, 1994.

Reference Works

Thomas, Dane. *Cross-Training for Expert Skiers: An Overview.* Powder Performance Center, Crested Butte, Colo., 1992.

U.S. Ski Team Alpine Training Manual. U.S. Ski Team, Park City, Utah, revised 1985.

U.S. Ski Team Media Guide. Park City, Utah, U.S. Ski Team, 1994.

Index

About the Author

Claudia Carbone started skiing during the 50s, when only a handful of ski areas existed in her native Colorado. High school friends took her to the top of Winter Park and urged her to follow. She's skied nearly every season since. Claudia writes a weekly ski column in Englewood and is published in numerous magazines and newspapers. She has received the North American Ski Journalists Association's highest award and was named Freelancer of the year by Colorado Ski Country USA.

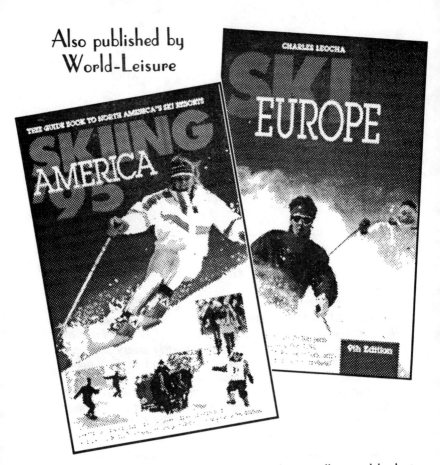